147610

P9-ECP-567

Sharpen Your Discernment

Sharpen Your Discernment:

Because When Life Looks Grey, It's Really Black and White

by
Roberts Liardon

ALBURY PUBLISHING
Tulsa, Oklahoma

Unless otherwise indicated, all Scripture quotations are taken from the *King James Version* of the Bible.

All Scripture quotations marked AMP are taken from *The Amplified New Testament*, copyright © 1958, 1987 by The Lockman Foundation, La Habra, California, or from *The Amplified Old Testament*, copyright © 1964, 1987 by Zondervan Publishing House, Grand Rapids, Michigan.

Sharpen Your Discernment: Because When Life Looks Grey, It's Really Black and White
ISBN 1-57778-029-9
Copyright © 1997 by Roberts Liardon
P. O. Box 30710
Laguna Hills, California 92654

Published by
ALBURY PUBLISHING
P. O. Box 470406
Tulsa, Oklahoma 74147-0406

Printed in the United States of America. All rights reserved under International Copyright Law. Contents and/or cover may not be reproduced in whole or in part in any form without the express written consent of the Publisher.

prophetic word

B y Roberts Liardon

February, 1995

Costa Mesa, California

"For one of the duties of the end-time servants, says the Lord, is that they have the ability to help people distinguish between that which is of Me, and that which is of them.

"For there are many who desire greater things of My Spirit, but have not been able to taste it or even see it, because of what's in them and on them and around them...it is not pure before Me, it is not right, and I cannot bring a greater glory to them. Because if I do, great trouble and turmoil will come to them.

"And I am looking, says the Spirit of God, for men and women who shall be able to divide for My people the right from the wrong, the holy from the profane, for it is important for the end-time Church to have this ability. And it is in a great need for this nation again to receive the difference and the understanding...of what is right and what is wrong.

"For even your society, says the Lord, has come to the place where those who walk your streets know not the difference between moral right and wrong.

"For it is so in the natural...how much greater is that so among them who call Me by My name, says the Lord.

"For there are many of them who walk around thinking that I am with them, and I am not. For there are many who say that I'm speaking through them, and I am not speaking through them.

"For I am ready to purify My people, and I am also ready to bring judgment upon them who willfully continue to make mockery of that which is holy, and that which is pure in the earth today.

"...For when hunger comes up from the inner man, oh, it does bring conviction on those who live in the mixtures of soul and spirit and have allowed evil to remain among them.

"And I am looking for a people who will call themselves to a new purity, and a new holiness, and a new life. A new life where I can walk through them strong and demonstrate My power in ways they have not seen.

"For [My people] have been the problem of what has limited My manifestations in the earth. For they themselves have not learned to discern the right from the wrong and to remain in the right, says the Spirit of the Lord.

"And know this day, I am trying to get into the hearts of My servants those things that are needful, where they'll be able to tell the difference, and to lead the people in the right direction, where there may be great joy within them and upon them.

"And there are so many who do sit around asking, 'Is this all? Is this what it is to be in the Spirit? Is this what it is to be in the glory?'"

"I've come to say to them, No, what you have tasted has been a mixture. And I am preparing, and I am moving through them who have listened, and them who have called out, to begin to bring the differentiation, the distinction, says the Spirit of God, between right and wrong.

"And oh, new joy shall come. Greater strength shall come, as the impurities and the falseness are removed and the soul takes its rightful place.

"For it is the time...says the Lord, to begin to ask, and to learn of Me in this way. For you have come this far. And now to go further, you must become more cunning, and more artful in the Spirit in how you walk. For every movement that you take, as you get higher, means more than you know and does more than you think.

"So knowing how to discern right from wrong, the right thing, and the wrong thing, will determine the purity of the move, the strength of your people, and the strength of your own heart, says the Spirit of the Lord.

"For there are those who have been offended, says the Spirit of God. They've been offended at how I planned to train them.

"Yes, they grew angry and offended when I corrected them, and they left their place of training. They left their place of divine training, says the Spirit of God, and for them to continue and to go forward, and to advance, they must come back to where they were offended and go through their offense and their training, says the Lord.

"For many do run, looking for a place to feel comfortable in their error, and I found a place where I can remove their error.

"And I will not chase you, for this operation comes by those who hunger and pursue Me of these things. So if you truly desire, says the Spirit of God, for these things to operate in you, then you must repent...For yes, you've developed your faith in healing, you've developed your faith in these things, but you have not developed an understanding of My Spirit's working so you can operate correctly in the weights of the glory that shall come.

"For yea, you cry, 'Oh, I want to see it. Oh, I want to be a part of it. Lord, use me,' you have said to Me many times. But yet you won't allow My preparational work to be done in you. For some want to know the knowledge but not have it done to them. For I will teach you by doing it to you, says the Lord. I will train you by taking you through these things.

"For some have run the other way to protect their ambition, and that is why their soul and their life are distraught. And oh, if you are true, says the Spirit of God, you'd truly, truly desire to have this operate strongly in you.

"Many of you must return to where you left, when I began to pull that which was not right out of your life and expose yourself to yourself. And oh, many men never come back. That's why there are so few who operate in some of the things that I've shown you, says the Spirit of the Lord.

"So let not deaf ears fall, but give ear to My Spirit, for I do desire, says the Holy Ghost...to impart unto you things that have been missing in your life and in your ministries. I do desire, says the Holy Ghost...I desire, I desire, I desire to give unto you abilities that are absent, abilities that are dormant I desire to awaken.

"I desire to remove the question from your life and put back the security, and knowings, and give you strength to carry on. For you are the ones who shall lead in the days ahead and not those who have allowed mixtures to become acceptable in their midst, says the Spirit of the Lord."

Appendix

As I completed this book, I felt led of the Lord to offer you some additional Scripture references to help you. I stated earlier that in my pastoral experiences, I've found the two major areas of confusion come in marriage and business.

These are not all the Scriptures pertaining to marriage and business, nor are they the total answer to your individual situation. But they will help to prepare a solid foundation upon which you can build your marriage and your business.

Choosing a Business Partner or a Business Deal

Whenever you are faced with knowing if a business deal or a partnership is of the Lord, compare the people involved and the business to these Scripture references:

The Book of Proverbs, especially Proverbs 1:10-19; Proverbs 24:1-4; Proverbs 23:17; Proverbs 12:24; Proverbs 10:4; Proverbs 12:27; Proverbs 13:4; Proverbs 21:5; Proverbs 13:20; Proverbs 29:3; Proverbs 22:26,27: Proverbs 17:18; Proverbs 11:15; Proverbs 6:1-5; Proverbs 22:13; Proverbs 20:4; Proverbs 14:23; Proverbs 25:19; Psalm 101:7; Ephesians 5:11; Psalm 1:3-6; Job 8:20; 1 Peter 4:12-15; 1 John 2:15-17; Acts 6:3; Acts 10:22; Acts 11:24; 1 Samuel 13:14; 1 Timothy 6:10; Psalm 26:9; 2 Corinthians 6:14; James 4:4; 1 Corinthians 5:11.

Choosing Your Mate

When you are seeking God's "best" in a lifetime mate, meditate upon these Scriptures:

The Book of Proverbs, especially Proverbs 1:5; Proverbs 13:20; Proverbs 29:3,11; Proverbs 26:12; Proverbs 25:28; Proverbs 17:28; Proverbs 7:4-27; Proverbs 6:32-35; Proverbs 4:23; Proverbs 28:7,24; Proverbs 21:19; Proverbs 14:17; Proverbs 22:24; Proverbs 29:22; Psalm 1:1-3; 2 Corinthians 6:14; 1 Corinthians 5:11; 1 Corinthians 6:13,18-20; 1 Corinthians 7:2-8; Galatians 5:19-21; 1 Thessalonians 4:3-5; Psalm 119:63; Psalm 27:14.

About the Author

Roberts Liardon is President of Roberts Liardon Ministries and Founder and Senior Pastor of Embassy Christian Center in Irvine, California. He is also Founder of Spirit Life Bible College and Life Ministerial Association in Irvine.

Roberts Liardon received his call to ministry as an eight-year-old boy. Since then, he has diligently endeavored to follow that call through preaching and teaching God's Word. He has preached in over eighty nations with extensive ministry in Europe, Asia, and Africa.

As a bestselling author, Roberts has expanded his ministry onto the printed page. His books have been translated into over twenty-seven languages and have been circulated throughout the world. Roberts books reflect his belief that the Church can fulfill its call and bring revival to the nations by combining God's Word with the moving of His Spirit.

As a historian, Roberts holds a wealth of knowledge regarding the great leaders of three Christian movements — Pentecostal, Divine Healing, and Charismatic. He embarked on his in-depth studies as a fourteen-year-old and continued those studies into adulthood. Roberts has established ongoing research through the founding of Reformers and Revivalist Historical Museum in California.

Roberts Liardon's television broadcast, *The High Life*, is aired weekly in Europe.

Other Books by Roberts Liardon

God's Generals

God's Generals Workbook

How to Survive an Attack

Religious Politics

The Invading Force

The Price of Spiritual Power

Learning to Say No Without Feeling Guilty

Run to the Battle

Kathryn Kuhlman

A Spiritual Biography of God's Miracle Working Power

Breaking Controlling Powers

Cry of the Spirit

Unpublished Sermons by Smith Wigglesworth

I Saw Heaven

A Call to Action

Spiritual Timing

The Quest for Spiritual Hunger

Forget Not His Benefits

Haunted Houses, Ghosts & Demons

Holding to the Word of the Lord

Additional copies of this book and other book titles from
ALBURY PUBLISHING are available at your local bookstore.

Albury Publishing
P. O. Box 470406
Tulsa, Oklahoma 74147-0406

In Canada books are available from:
Word Alive
P. O. Box 670
Niverville, Manitoba
CANADA ROA 1EO

Spirit Life Bible College

Spirit Life Bible College is a teaching center and a spiritual hub where men and women of God come to be equipped, developed, and strengthened to fulfill the plan of God for this generation. From every status in life, all over the world, those who dare to answer the call of God come to SLBC and are transformed into the revivalists and reformers of this day and age. Whether their call is in the marketplace or in the world of ministry, these men and women of destiny invade the territories of the world, assured of fulfilling their high call.

SLBC Will Equip the Cry of Your Heart!

*For more information, or to receive
a catalog and application, please contact
the international office nearest you.*

In the USA call:

(714) 833-3555

or write:

Spirit Life Bible College
P. O. Box 30710
Laguna Hills, CA 92654-0710

Roberts Liardon Ministries International Offices:

Europe
Roberts Liardon Ministries
P. O. Box 2043
Hove, Brighton
East Sussex, BN3 6JU England
Phone and Fax: 44 1273 777427

South Africa
Roberts Liardon Ministries
P. O. Box 3155
Kimberly 8300, South Africa
Phone and Fax: 27 531 82 1207

USA
Roberts Liardon Ministries
P. O. Box 30710
Laguna Hills, California 92654
Phone: (714) 833-3555
Fax: (714) 833-9555

Contents

241
L6130

LIFE Pacific College
Alumni Library
1100 West Covina Blvd.
San Dimas, CA 91773

048811

chapter one

2 + 2 = 4

"*Two plus two is four, Roberts.*"

Years ago, I was minding my own business when those words boomed in my spirit. It totally caught me by surprise. I had been asking the Lord for an answer to a certain situation that was troubling me, but I never expected to hear such simplicity, much less a math equation! I thought the answer to my problem would be complicated, so I tried to ignore what I was hearing.

But it didn't ignore me. It didn't go away. In fact, it didn't matter what I was doing. I heard that simple, abrupt sentence everywhere I went! It didn't matter if I'd just preached in a dynamic service where God had moved tremendously, or if I was driving down the highway. It didn't matter if I was in an intense and demanding situation, or if I was just brushing my teeth! Out of the blue it would interrupt my daily life, challenging me to hear it's truth, "*Two plus two is four.*"

I'd go into my office, and right in the middle of dictating a letter or answering a phone call, I'd hear in my spirit, "*Two plus two is four.*"

I kept thinking, "What is this?" At times, it seemed funny. Yet I kept asking the Lord for the answer to my complicated problem. And over and over that sentence would pop up in my spirit.

"*Two plus two is four.*"

Finally, after a month of constantly hearing the Lord repeat Himself, I replied, "Well, Lord, I know that."

He said, *"Then quit adding an extra point because you're familiar with people."*

During this time, I'd had two preacher friends that I thought would be great friends to each other. So I had introduced them — but they became the worst of enemies! Not only were they enemies, but soon they began to pull on me to take sides! It was a mess.

Now that might not seem dramatic to you, but it was to me. I really liked both of these people. Relationships are very important to me, and I couldn't believe that my good intentions had ended so badly. In fact, the situation bothered me so much that I began second-guessing my discernment.

If the devil can ever rob you of spiritual knowings, then you are left confused and defenseless.

It was during this time that the Lord began ministering to me in a very elementary way. He used a simple math equation to illustrate a startling point: *Two plus two is four, not five.* I liked my two friends. And because of that, I was adding an extra point to our relationship, covering over the things that I didn't want to see. By doing that, I began to have problems with my own discernment.

I can look back in my ministry, and every time we had a problem with anyone in my private life or public life, it was because I overrode what I knew in my spirit. I would see things by the Spirit, and then say, "No, that's not really there. I'll ignore it. I'm sure it'll go away." But it didn't go away. I compromised with what I saw because I enjoyed the relationship. And pretty soon, the thing that I ignored would come up and bite me!

If you cover up a problem and fail to deal with what God has shown you, then one day or another, the problem will come back around and end up biting you too. You'll end up hurt and disappointed, blaming God and everyone else, thinking you can't trust anyone. But the whole problem is in your own personal discernment, and your failure to respond to what the Spirit of God is showing you.

Do you have a good friend you really love, and this friend is doing something totally contrary to the will of God for his or her life? Perhaps this person is getting into error, or making a decision that will cause terrible problems down the road. Have you spoken to them according to what you've discerned? Or are you just ignoring it, choosing the way of silence because you fear confrontation? It's better to be right with God than to be found among the dumb and the blind!

Whatever you lay down with will get on you. In other words, if you start ignoring error and stupidity, then pretty soon we'll be calling you by those same names. Your wall of spiritual strength will be broken down by what you willfully accept or ignore.

It sounds humorous, but spiritual discernment was given to keep you from being bit and to help you follow the truth. If you hold to discernment, you'll come out on top, no matter what it looks like. If you disregard it, you'll be a playground for the devil.

Are you being bit by what you didn't follow through on several months or even years ago? Maybe you're the pastor of a church and God has given you a specific direction for your congregation. But because you fear the results, or the people, or the political regime of your particular denomination, you've ignored Him. What you're actually saying is that God is not your Source. He is not the Director of your life and ministry. If you work for

Him, your instructions must come from Him. If not, you'll end up getting bit!

Have you been shown something by the Spirit of God and you've discredited it? This is especially true with business people who are ruled by greed and money. These are the ones who drop their standards to hire someone who'll make money for them.

I know of a wonderful Christian business that started out bringing glory to the Lord. Their staff was carefully chosen and prayed over. But now they've risen as a star in the competitive public eye and have been swayed by greed. They've hired someone who is in deep sexual perversion and have given the person a high position. Why? Because this person is skilled and has an ability to bring in money. The leaders of this business have totally discredited the warnings in their spirits. They think if this perverted moral problem is ignored, it won't bite them. It's sad, but unless they repent and correct themselves, the writing is on the wall.

How do people make such terrible mistakes? How can some be called the righteousness of God and act so dumb and foolish? Why does someone marry the wrong person? Why do Christians find themselves in crazy business deals and end up losing everything?

Why does a person hear the Lord, then discount it? What does it mean when you think you've heard from the Lord, and everything ends in chaos? Or why do some people open themselves up to anything that seems spiritual?

I'm going to answer those questions in this book. I don't pretend to have all the answers; but this book is a good place for you to start in your search for discernment. If you'll read it and hunger to walk in truth, then you'll have a hard time missing God.

2 + 2 = 4, Not 3

In my hunger to understand spiritual discernment, the Lord gave me another principle. I had just recovered from a drastic mistake by learning the first 2 + 2 principle, and out of the blue here comes another one!

One day I heard the Lord say, *"Roberts, two plus two is four, not **three**."*

Realizing how slow I had been before, this time I caught on! I began to seek the Lord and examine my life. Obviously, I had miscalculated somewhere.

Then I saw it.

Just as I realized that I was adding an extra point because I liked a person, I was also taking points away because I wasn't seeing a person by the Spirit.

Here's what I mean. I had an evangelist friend. I had ministered with this person several times. But here's the truth: Though I liked this person, his method of ministry made me feel chaotic and out of order! Yes, the gifts of the Spirit operated accurately through this ministry, and the doctrine was fine. But the method made me search for my last nerve!

When my friend ministered, a group of people would be reacting in one spot, while another group would be carrying on in a different place. People would be sporadically walking around the building, and some came up on the platform. My friend would be running to this spot, then over to that spot, preaching here and there and everywhere. I found myself standing in a corner, numb!

Now understand, that was his method and it worked. It was fine with God. But it wasn't my method, and I had a problem with it.

One portion of my call is to operate prophetically. I must know what is happening and have people ready to assist so that I can continue hearing clearly. If several things are happening in the Spirit — healings, salvations, deliverances, etc. — I sometimes appoint people to handle the different areas so I can focus on the main thing.

Evangelists don't operate that way. Usually, they are spectacular and are not pleased unless a variety of things are happening all at once in every corner of the building!

Until I understood that this method of ministry was fine with God, I was uneasy with it. In fact, I wanted to stop ministering with this evangelist because I so uncomfortable. We had a great friendship; I just wanted to be in another city when he ministered in mine! And that's when I heard the next life-changing equation of *two plus two is four, not three.*

By cutting off a particular administration because I didn't operate that way, I was severing an important relationship that God had given me. I was allowing my personal preferences to rule over the ways of God.

There are churches and people today who won't hear anyone unless the minister is a teacher. They like teaching, so they overdose on every Greek and Hebrew word that's available. Then there are those who run to the prophets, and so on. Can you imagine how these people must look in the Spirit? I like ice cream, but what if that's all I ate? My body would be sadly lacking in protein, fat, vitamins and minerals. I'd be one walking, talking carbohydrate!

We can apply this humorous principle to the Spirit. God gave us all of the five-fold ministries — apostle, prophet, teacher, pastor, and evangelist — to fulfill and provide us with the spiritual nutrients to make us strong, well-rounded believers. If we allow our personal preferences to pick and choose the gifts we like, we'll be deficient in some area.

At that particular time in my life, I was tired of missing the vital relationships that I needed. However, I thought these relationships would fit my personal preferences. Through another simple math equation, God began to help me relax and receive what He had placed in my life.

God doesn't intend for you to be rigid and uptight. One of the key attributes of His kingdom is peace. When you learn to see after the Spirit, you'll always live in peace. As we progress in this book, I'm going to teach you how to see people after the Spirit so you won't be found in a miscalculated deficit.

Why Do We Need It?

I've traveled all over the world and am very familiar with the moves of God throughout the churches. There is a strong stirring in the realm of the spirit, and the Church is witnessing a greater power, a greater fire, and a greater glory throughout the earth. But there are also greater counterfeits to oppose.

The sad part is, some Christians can't tell the difference between the work of God and the work of the flesh or demonic power. Or, if they do recognize it, many don't know what to do about it.

Throughout all my travels, whether ministering behind the pulpit, in counseling, or in prayer lines, I've found the number one problem in the Church is *the lack of spiritual discernment.*

Many Christians have developed themselves in the truths of healing, deliverance, and prosperity. That's wonderful, but they've stopped there. Besides healing, deliverance, salvation, and prosperity, Jesus did even more for us. He sent the Holy Spirit to the earth with a mission to remain with us until we leave here.

It is the mission of the Holy Spirit to equip and undergird you, to strengthen and guide you into all truth. He will tell you what is happening, how it's happening, and many times why it's happening.

Yet many Christians have never even thought about developing their spiritual awareness to the Person of the Holy Spirit. They've never given much thought on how to work with His leadings and direction in order to fine-tune their lives. In fact, many don't even know that they have discernment or that it is a part of their spiritual equipment. They have the Forrest Gump mentality that life is like a box of chocolates: You never know what you're going to get.

Then there are Christians who only look to the media, or to books, or to certain magazines to find out what God is doing. It's disastrous if those same Christians think that the featured author or the most publicized personality is the one with all the answers for the hour.

No, no, no, NO!

Many Christians think discernment only operates through the five-fold ministry — pastor, teacher, evangelist, prophet or apostle. Some even think that there is a ministry of discernment, and if a believer operates in discernment, that person is highly gifted.

Again, *no!* If you think that way, it's no wonder you're living from crisis to crisis.

We've all been given the same spiritual equipment, but it seems only some know how to activate it. Some know how to work with it. It is the will of God for *every* believer to know how their discernment equipment operates.

Before we go on, ask yourself these questions and take the time to evaluate your discernment. Do you know when the Holy Spirit has come into the room? When He comes into the room, can you discern what He wants to do? Do you know how to honor and work with His presence? Can you discern between the flesh and the Spirit? The profane and the holy? If you can, do you know what to do about it?

Know this day that God is searching for those who have learned the art of spiritual discernment. He is looking for the ones who have sought to know the Holy Spirit and for those who allow the Spirit of God to work strongly through them.

The love of God is unconditional, but His blessings aren't. Those who have sought to know the Holy Spirit and the spiritual equipment they've been given are the ones who will demonstrate His power in ways the earth has never seen. It is those men and women who will be able to change the hearts of their nation, to lead the people in the right direction, that there may be great joy before the coming of the Lord.

That's why I'm writing this book. Years ago, I came to the point where I was frustrated at seeing my friends and others making dumb decisions, marrying the wrong people, and failing at business ventures. I watched helplessly as they collapsed and crumbled. I was pinpointing the problem *after* the facts; but I needed to know the answers *before* the problems began. As I searched, God began to help me.

It didn't happen overnight. It took a sequence of trying and testing my discernment and finding it was correct. As I began to trust and mature my spiritual equipment, I became confident in what I was hearing. Then I began to speak out and end disastrous situations before they could manifest and destroy my life and the lives of others. Mature discernment is a spiritual progression, and you must be willing to start at the first point.

God will teach you spiritual discernment by working it through you and building upon each lesson. For example, if I showed you a gun, I could tell you all about the mechanics and operations of that piece of equipment. But that's only a partial knowledge.

If you needed to use that gun, knowledge alone wouldn't cause you to hit the bull's eye. No, only experience with and knowledge of that gun would cause you to hit the target.

Spiritual discernment operates the same way. Knowledge, along with actual hands-on training, produce accuracy.

As you read, I'm going to show you how to discern between the Spirit of God and the moves of the flesh and the devil. You'll see how to discern between spiritual mixtures and the purity of God. I'll give you some practical illustrations and even some bizarre ones. I want you to understand how to use what you've discerned, the differences between spiritual discernment and soulish discernment, and how to biblically test a spirit. You'll learn when to speak out, when to keep quiet, and when to run. When you finish this book, I believe you'll have a good, overall understanding of how spiritual discernment operates.

Spiritual discernment will strengthen you, assure you, and equip you. It's just waiting for you to activate it. If you'll apply the wisdom and experience that I'm going to share with you, then you'll understand discernment and you'll never lose it.

the basis of accurate discernment

Your personal experiences, godly counsel, and the Word of God each play a vital role in your discernment ability. Let's look briefly at each of these three areas.

A. Discernment By Experience

We've all heard parents say of their children, "I wish they would listen to me and not have to learn the hard way." It's true that wisdom would be the best way to learn, but most of us learn our lessons from experience. If I've had an experience with something, good or bad, I discern from that experience in the future.

However, there is a warning that comes with experience. Just as you can use your past experiences to better yourself, those same experiences can also cause you to miss out or withdraw in fear.

Some of us have had terrible experiences in the course of life. We must allow God to fully heal those wounds inside of us. The healing won't always come by spiritual counsel. If we think that way, we will be greatly disappointed. Many times, God Himself will have to supernaturally intervene in our life and help us to understand why a situation happened, or what caused it. When God speaks, the situation is forever settled.

If the experience was devastating, it may take some time for you to sort everything out. And that's fine. If you continue on with God, knowing Him and serving Him to your best ability, you'll find yourself healed, matured, and invaluable to the body of Christ.

How can you tell if a past experience remains unhealed and is dominant in your mind? It's easy to tell. Do you run from the first indication of something that reminds you of the past?

Sometimes a person may be having a bad day and they may say or do something that reminds you of a terrible experience. If you blast them or withdraw in fear, then your past experience is still holding you. If you discern a temporary situation based solely on your horrible experience, then you've not progressed in that area.

Learn to patiently watch and hear. Be careful not to over-react. Many times, things are not always as they appear to be. Just because something might remind you of the past doesn't mean your present situation will be identical to it. Seldom do devastating life experiences happen more than once, unless the person blindly enters into it.

When people are always thinking and watching for the bad, they can enter into spiritual error. Trying to pad themselves from further hurt, they enter into areas where they are not called, or begin to operate in familiar spirits. Sometimes a Jezebel spirit, which is highly controlling, can attach itself. The broken person thinks if they can control everything, hurt will not come.

Don't allow your past to cause you to set yourself up in an ivory tower or cower in a cave somewhere. Relax and allow your past to work for you — not against you. The Spirit of God knows how to walk you into total victory.

The Positive Side

On the positive side, experiences can also bring strength and faith for a greater feat. We can read an example of this in the Old Testament. As a young boy, past experiences certainly strengthened David. From conquering everyday situations as a shepherd, such as protecting his sheep from lions and other prey, he gained the discernment and trust to take on a larger project — namely, Goliath.

In First Samuel, chapter 17, we can read the story. Saul and his army of Israelites were hiding in the trenches at the valley of Elah. They had hoped to defeat the Philistines but were tragically sent into an array.

The scene was dramatic. Here were two opposing armies encamped in valleys on the opposite sides of a huge plain. On one side, the Philistines were riotous and unruly, while on the other side the Israelites were cowering and shaking with fear.

In the middle of the two valleys, standing almost ten feet tall, was the Philistine champion named Goliath. Upon his massive head was a helmet of bronze. Strapped across his chest, back, and shoulders was a scaled coat of bronzed armor, weighing in at two hundred pounds. He had bronzed shields covering both his legs, and the iron head of his spear weighed twenty-five pounds. If that wasn't enough, Goliath also had a shield-bearer who went out before him.

Goliath stood in the plain spewing out slander and threats towards the Israelites. Laughingly he mocked God and them, promising nothing less than death and slavery for the price of their blood.

Suddenly a little shepherd boy named David came on the scene, carrying food to his brothers in the Israeli service. As he approached, David expected to see a heated battle taking place. Instead, what he saw and how he reacted would forever change the history of the world.

Listening to the verbal abuse of Goliath, David was enraged. He asked the army of Israel who this uncircumcised Philistine was who dared to threaten the armies of God.

His embarrassed and anxious brother rebuked him. But David answered in a way that separates the boys of God from the men of God. In verse 29 he replied to his brother, *"Is there not a cause?"*

Experience With a Cause

David might have been a young boy, but he had purpose to his life. When David showed up situations changed, because he had a cause. Everything he did and every job he performed, David did with divine purpose. Because of this spiritual understanding, David made every experience work to his benefit. Behind every experience, it is the cause, it is the purpose — or lack of it — that makes a person become better or bitter.

It was that cause which strengthened David as he stood in the face of Saul and declared:

> Let no man's heart fail because of him [Goliath]...Thy servant kept his father's sheep, and there came a lion, and a bear, and took a lamb out of the flock:
>
> And I went out after him, and smote him, and delivered it out of his mouth: and when he arose against me, I caught him by his beard, and smote him, and slew him.
>
> Thy servant slew both the lion and the bear: and this uncircumcised Philistine shall be as one of them, seeing he hath defied the armies of the living God.
>
> 1 Samuel 17:32,34-36

Then David loosed his experience to do the talking:

20

The Lord that delivered me out of the paw of the lion, and out of the paw of the bear, he will deliver me out of the hand of this Philistine.

Verse 37

Saul was defenseless, as all causeless people are. All he could mutter was, *"Go, and the Lord be with thee"* (v. 37).

Saul offered David his armor, but David refused. He took only what he knew would work.

Can you see this dramatic scene?

Out of the trenches came a small, unarmed boy, ready to meet the hulk. In response, Goliath laughed and cursed David by his heathen gods. But his gods were probably smarter than Goliath and had already run off!

Goliath bellowed, "Come to me and I'll feed your flesh to the birds and the beasts." Goliath's stature was nearly ten feet tall, but David's words measured higher! To his threat David roared:

...I come to thee in the name of the Lord of hosts, the God of the armies of Israel, whom thou hast defied.

This day will the Lord deliver thee into mine hand; and I will smite thee, and take thine head from thee; and I will give the carcases of the host of the Philistines this day unto the fowls of the air, and to the wild beasts of the earth; that all the earth may know that there is a God in Israel.

...for the battle is the Lord's, and he will give you into our hands.

1 Samuel 17:45-47

At David's challenge, Goliath stood and walked towards him. But it was too late for intimidation! David's past experiences had clothed him in supernatural strength. Discerning a sure victory, David ran towards his enemy. With one sure shot, a stone was hurled from his sling.

The stone deeply embedded Goliath's skull. Before the hulk could even blink, he dropped dead at the hand of a boy with a cause. When the rest of the Philistine army saw this supernatural feat, they kicked up their heels and ran for their lives!

Experience is a great discerner for victory. Don't allow your experiences to defeat you. Even if your past was bad, turn it into the wisdom of God. Then you'll have a cause or a purpose to stand for the right. If the same ugly experience tries to bellow and roar against you, apply what you've learned. Don't cower and withdraw as one with no hope. Allow a godly cause to bring you strength. Then discern your steps and run towards the victory!

B. Discernment and Godly Counsel

Sometimes we can't see the right way to go. The Bible says in Proverbs 11:14:

> **Where no counsel is, the people fall: but in the multitude of counsellors there is safety.**

However, this verse carries a hidden responsibility on your part: **Make sure your counselors are spiritually mature and alert.** In this particular verse, the Hebrew meaning for the word *counselor* means to "advise, determine, guide,"[1] and here's that word again, "purpose."

We all have a different plan and purpose for our lives, so make sure your counselor is alert to that fact. Don't go to what I call a "generic counselor," or someone who counsels everyone in the same way. And be careful of the ones who don't have a clear understanding of how God operates. In the Book of Job, you'll read how Job sought the wrong counsel and ended up blaming God for all his problems.

Seek out the ones who are spiritually sensitive and have an insight into your specific calling. While there are basic fundamental truths that apply to all of us, you can't counsel an evangelist the same way you'd counsel a prophet. You can't always counsel someone in the business world like you'd counsel one in the ministry.

While seeking the divine counsel you need, you may have some "hits and misses." How will you know? It's simple. If you don't have your answer or if you are unable to see your way clearly, then you counseled with the wrong person. God is not complicated. Once you've had the Spirit-led counsel from heaven, you'll be able to discern the difference.

The Amplified Version of Proverbs 1:5 says that the person who chooses proper and divine counsel is a person of understanding. Skill and direction are promised to them.

The wise also will hear and increase in learning, and the person of understanding will acquire skill and attain to sound counsel [so that he may be able to steer his course rightly].

If you seek counsel for discernment, then find the person who is divinely sensitive and experienced to the call for your life. They'll counsel you from that purpose and direction. Then you'll be able to discern your way.

There's a rule I use for pursuing personal counsel. Usually, the best counsel I receive is from someone who is older, more mature, and more experienced. When I need counsel those are the first ones I seek out. The second best counsel is from someone who is on the same spiritual level, with equal sensitivity.

Understand that once you've found the Spirit-led counsel that's needed, you have a responsibility to heed their wisdom.

I'll say it another way. If you've placed yourself under a godly pastor and he gives you Spirit-led counsel, then you are obligated to recognize that counsel as discernment for your life. If you don't agree with his counsel, then make sure he is aware of every detail that causes you to disagree. If you've presented the details and the counsel remains the same, you are obligated to heed the discernment. If not, then be forewarned of the consequences.

Understand what I'm saying. I know there is some error with shepherding doctrines, specifically where the pastor is given total control over the daily lives of his congregation. I'm not talking about throwing your daughter out of the house because the pastor doesn't agree with the person she's about to marry. I'm certainly not saying that the pastor should dictate to your family.

The pastor is not there to control your life. The choice to follow is still yours. The pastor is to bring light where there's darkness. He or she is given to you as an instrument to shape and mold your life so you can fulfill the plan of God. The pastor is to give you that discernment, then release you to make a choice.

In my years of pastoring, I've found that the two main mistakes people make are in marriage and business. In fact, I almost entitled this book, *How Not To Marry an Idiot and Do Business With a Crook*.

Over and over I've seen people get themselves with the wrong people. Then when they decide it's time to seek the will of God, they're already emotionally married. By that time, it's usually too late. We've already lost them.

Or, they get all excited about some business deal. But when they start listening to the warnings in their spirits, they've already signed on the dotted line. Those people suffer years of financial hardships. Some collapse and lose everything. Know this — Scripture does not support "get-rich-quick" schemes. In fact, Proverbs outlines the types of people to do business with, and the ones to stay away from.

Here's a personal example of pastoring and Spirit-led counseling that might help you. There was a couple in my church who were faithful and seemed to be strong for the Lord. Both were sharp, well-groomed, beautiful people training for the ministry. He held a prominent ministry of helps position and she was in Bible school.

This couple began to date, and suddenly presented themselves for marriage. I believed the marriage was of the Lord and felt they would be a great couple, having a wonderful life. But something was just a little off. There was something not quite right.

All of sudden, another guy began to get interested in the girl. The man in my church flew off the handle and wanted to report this other guy to the police. He felt the guy was harassing his girlfriend. When I heard of it, my spirit yelled, "Whoa!" Then I was able to label the little problem that I had discerned.

I called the man in for counseling and asked him to wait about six months before they married. I told him that the Spirit of the Lord had shown me that he had a spirit of anger and rage. God wanted him to be free of it before they married. If not, it would warp and control his wife and she wouldn't be free to be the woman she wanted to be. Eventually, abusive treatment could happen because he wouldn't be happy with himself or what his control had caused her to be.

I further told him that he was rushing the marriage because he was afraid he would lose this girl. I had no doubt that the two should be married, but I encouraged him to wait for six months and allow himself to be freed of the spirit of anger which he had tried to hide.

The man praised me to my face, then slandered me behind my back. He stated that he would not place my counsel over his marriage or ministry.

Do you see how deceptive that was? The man didn't have either — a marriage or a ministry! He was serving in the ministry of helps as a single man, and the girl was emotionally gone. One "I love you" from this man made her deaf to any Spirit-led discernment.

It was a very sad day for me when the couple left my ministry to pursue a more accommodating leadership. In a pastoral position, the counsel I gave was not my mere opinion. I had heard from the Lord, Who had revealed the very secrets of the man's heart, yet he would not hear my counsel nor count it as discernment. The discernment was given to strengthen his life and to groom him. Yet as his pastor, I had to stand with the word of the Lord and allow him to make a choice. He made the choice and left.

If the guy felt himself to be ready for marriage, then God held him accountable for the direction of his future family. I believe that every decision a man makes will affect his wife and children. As a leader of the family, the man must be willing to make the right choices. If not, the family will suffer. Righteous suffering is a joy, but suffering by stupidity is grief. God wanted to start this man on the right road, but he refused to hear.

No man is an island to himself. Only a fool would hear divine counsel from heaven and throw it to the wind.

The Book of Daniel records what happened to such a fool.

The Bible, the Counsel, and the Fool

In Daniel, chapter four, King Nebuchadnezzar had been troubled by a dream. He called for all his magicians and psychics, asking them to interpret it. But no one could interpret the dream to satisfy him.

Finally, the king called for Daniel. Before telling him of the dream, the king acknowledged that the Spirit of God dwelt with Daniel. Based on that understanding, the king asked Daniel to interpret the dream.

Well, Daniel's interpretation didn't fit what the king wanted to hear. He proceeded to tell the king that his kingdom would be brought low and that he himself would be as the beasts of the field, because he had taken the credit for his greatness instead of giving the glory to God. Then Daniel pleaded:

> Therefore, O king, let my counsel be acceptable to you; break off your sins and show the reality of your repentance by righteousness (right standing with God and moral and spiritual rectitude and rightness in every area and relation)...that [if the king will repent] there may possibly be a continuance and lengthening of your peace and tranquility and a healing of your error.
>
> Daniel 4:27 AMP

Nebuchadnezzar didn't repent. Instead, he went on his way, pretending the dream never happened.

One year later, the king stood in his palace and boasted of how great Babylon was because of him. At that very hour, the consequences of the dream came to pass. Nebuchadnezzar was driven out of the palace and into the pasture to eat grass with the oxen. For seven years he was out of his mind.

Then one day Nebuchadnezzar turned his eyes towards heaven. At that moment his understanding returned and he blessed the Lord as the Most High God Who ruled the kingdoms of the earth. Once he repented, Nebuchadnezzar's kingdom was returned with more greatness than before. He spent the rest of his days blessing and honoring the King of Heaven.

Had Nebuchadnezzar followed the divine counsel for his life Daniel had offered, he would not have suffered the consequences for seven long years.

When you hear from God, **follow it.**

Now there are times when no counselor is available to help you. If you know and understand your covenant with God, you're never at a loss. All you have to do is activate that covenant. The Spirit of Counsel has been given to us, and we can always draw from that spiritual insight and discern our way. In Isaiah 11, the Old Testament prophet foretold of the anointings that would rest upon Jesus.

> And the spirit of the Lord shall rest upon him, the spirit of wisdom and understanding, the spirit of counsel and might, the spirit of knowledge and of the fear of the Lord;
>
> And shall make him of quick understanding in the fear of the Lord: and he shall not judge after the sight of his eyes, neither reprove after the hearing of his ears.
>
> Isaiah 11:2,3

If Jesus Christ is your Savior, then the same Spirit that rested upon Him is now available to you.

Many times in counseling sessions, I may not have the answers. As the person is speaking to me, I call upon the Spirit of Counsel to give me supernatural wisdom and insight so that I may discern the situation before me. Without fail, the wisdom of God always comes to meet the need of the moment. Why? Because I activate one of my rights in the kingdom of God. I call upon the Spirit of Counsel to help me and the answers come.

Know this: If you seek direction and discernment, God will make sure you find your way.

C. Discernment With the Word

There is the basic discernment that we can get from the Bible. In fact, *the Word of God is the basis for all discernment.*

You will never know God or understand the situations of life aside from the Bible. Within the Word are the principles and the character of God. Once we learn it, the Word will help us to discern the situations we face.

At times you may not be able to properly discern the circumstances before you. If so, then open the Word, read it, and find your answer. I think sometimes people think in order to discern things, they must receive a spectacular revelation. They don't use what they have because it doesn't seem spectacular. But when your Word level is full, you'll discern people and situations. It'll just pop out of you, because the Word of God will label it.

You don't need a vision, a spiritual feeling, or a spectacular event to discern with the Word. The Word is clear as it describes people and situations. When you agree with it, you're not being judgmental or critical. You're simply labeling what the Word has already judged.

How does the Word discern? Scriptures will label a person by stating how the person will act, how they will dress, or how they will conduct their lives. You can be sure of your discernment simply because the Bible states it as a fact.

Proverbs is a wonderful book for describing or defining the character of every man or woman. If someone is acting a certain way, open the Book of Proverbs and read what it says about that type of behavior. Virtuous women, frugal people, liberal people, the sluggard, the diligent, the furious, wise behavior, foolish behavior — it's all there, as well as the outcome of such behavior.

For example, let's read Proverbs 7. Look at how the first two verses begin:

My son, keep my words, and lay up my commandments with thee.

Keep my commandments, and live....

In other words, if you discern by what these verses tell you and strongly live by them, then you'll live in peace and understanding. If you don't, deception will ensnare you.

It goes on in verse 5:

That they may keep thee from the strange woman, from the stranger which flattereth with her words.

In this generation, you have to watch for both strange women *and* men. Then we have some who don't know what they are, male or female. But according to Proverbs, their mannerisms and outcomes are all the same.

The chapter goes on to describe how a loose person, or a person with a seductive spirit, behaves. They dress in a certain way, they're lewd and show nakedness, they're loud and stubborn, and their feet abide not in their own houses.

Now when the Word starts defining things like that and you retain it, then you'll recognize it when it exists in someone. If the Word labels it, then you label it.

There are some people you can just look at and identify their lifestyle. You don't need glasses. It's right there in front of you, so just call it what it is. Don't try to make a show of them. Just know how to discern it within yourself.

You might say, "Well, Roberts, I don't want to be cruel."

I didn't say, "Be cruel." I'm saying, "Run! Run!" If the Word defines it, you'd better do the same.

If you don't know the Word, you'll never be able to discern accurately.

For example, if you don't know what the Bible says about a fool, then go through the Bible and find out about the subject. Get a concordance and write down everything the Word of God says about a fool. Learn what a fool says, what a fool does, and the reward of a fool. Then when you meet one, you'll know it!

Discernment with the Bible works like this: When the Word of God is inside your heart, the Holy Spirit will cause it to come to your consciousness when you need it.

Whenever you are faced with a business deal, an opportunity, or circumstance, the Holy Spirit will walk with you and cause a certain verse to come to your remembrance. Or, He might bring to mind a biblical character or a Bible incident.

When the Holy Spirit operates through one of these areas, research the verse or the character. Look at your own situation and discern it. Sometimes you may just recall a fragment of something you've read. Quickly get to a Bible and read the whole story. The Holy Spirit is speaking to you.

Analyze what you've recalled. How did that biblical character operate? What does the Bible say to do about that? If they did it in the Word, then you should do it too. That's how God helps you, using what you've put inside of yourself.

Sometimes when we get in a mess, we say, "Well, the Lord tried to tell me, but I didn't quite get it."

If you didn't get it, you didn't take the time to get it.

Hebrews 4:12 assures us that the Word will give us the ability to cut and divide — or discern — situations facing us. It says:

For the word of God is quick, and powerful, and sharper than any twoedged sword, piercing even to the dividing asunder of soul and spirit...and is a discerner of the thoughts and intents of the heart.

If you allow the Holy Spirit to work with you in this fashion, the Word will cut through the clouds and divide the confusion. You'll be able to see what's happening and what motivated a certain type of action. That's the operation of spiritual discernment.

---

[1] *Strong's Exhaustive Concordance of the Bible*, #8458. (MacDonald Publishing Company; McLean, VA)

the gift of discerning of spirits

The gift of discerning of spirits is described in First Corinthians 12.

Most people think that's the only type of discernment there is, and that it's only for a certain group of people. But the gift of discerning of spirits comes as all the other gifts do. You do not own it, but when the need demands it, the Holy Spirit supernaturally manifests this gift through you to remedy the situation at hand.

The gift of discerning of spirits is just what it says. Notice that the word "spirits" is plural. There are several spirits to discern. There are demons, angels, the human spirit, and the Spirit of God. So this gift was not only given to discern evil, but to discern the good as well.

Some people think the gifts of the Spirit can only operate in a church service or an evangelistic meeting. But the gifts of the Spirit will help you in counseling, in soulwinning, and out on the streets in day-to-day situations.

In the sixteenth chapter of the Book of Acts, we can read where this gift operated during a street incident. Paul operated in the gift of discerning of spirits and cast out an evil spirit. *The Amplified Version* states:

> As we were on our way to the place of prayer, we were met by a slave girl who was possessed by a spirit of divination [claiming to foretell future events and to discover hidden knowledge], and she brought her owners much gain by her fortunetelling.

She kept following Paul and [the rest of] us, shouting loudly, These men are the servants of the Most High God! They announce to you the way of salvation!

And she did this for many days. Then Paul, being sorely annoyed and worn out, turned and said to the spirit within her, I charge you in the name of Jesus Christ to come out of her! And it came out that very moment.

Acts 16:16-18 AMP

I love these verses! You'd better know that psychics, horoscope writers, and fortune-tellers are all motivated by the spirit of divination and the occult. A demon spirit, or several of them, are behind it all no matter how religious the person may act. In fact, many will attempt to act religious to sway the foolish and undiscerning. You'd be surprised how many clueless people go to church, yet read their daily horoscope or watch the Psychic Network.

Paul knew his righteous covenant with God. Notice the Word doesn't state that Paul was afraid or concerned by this demon spirit. Instead, Scripture says Paul was annoyed. The constant harping of this demon began to wear on the spirit of Paul, so he turned around and dealt with the nuisance once and for all. He discerned the spirit motivating her and cast it out for all to see. Paul operated in the gift of discerning of spirits.

In my book, *God's Generals, Why They Succeeded and Why Some Failed,* I tell of story after story where men and women of God discerned the presence of Jesus coming into a room and healing the sick. There are also stories of holy angels being seen protecting the man or woman of God from dangerous, unruly crowds. That's the gift of discerning of spirits in operation. You need to read these true accounts of history to gain a better understanding of what's available to you as well.

There are many, many stories my grandmother, Gladoylene "Gram" Moore, tells of how the gifts of discerning of spirits operated through her. At times she would be sent by God into certain meetings so He could show her what was operating. She would pray the spirits off the minister, and afterwards the meeting would be over! False evangelists would run out of town because they were caught.

While I was growing up, education was very important in my family, but it seemed like the gifts of the Spirit and the operations of God were stressed every waking moment! When my sister and I were old enough to go to school, we would come home at the end of the day to meet my grandmother at the front door. She would lay hands all over us, praying in wild tongues and casting anything off that we might have picked up during the day. It worked!

You can operate in the gift of discerning of spirits as well. All you need to do is reach out, be easily yielded, and let the Spirit of God know you're available for Him to speak through and help someone.

Many years ago I spoke with a great saint. I was about sixteen years old when I met her. She had worked with Aimee Semple McPherson and had helped E. W. Kenyon in his ministry.

I was just a young guy, and she loved young preachers. She said, "I want to give you a piece of advice that will keep your counseling volume low." She told me that if I would tap into the gifts of the Spirit, the problems that normally took years to solve could be settled within minutes.

The Holy Spirit will never shove His gifts upon you. He's a gentleman, and He'll wait to see if you want them. So cry out for the gifts of the Spirit to come to you!

And when they come, just allow the Spirit of God to speak through you. Don't get religious. Be yourself and speak. If you'll do that, then some problems will be solved very quickly. There are some things around you now that could be instantly solved if you'd only tap into what's available to you!

daily discernment

Thank God we can receive the gifts of the Spirit when they're needed, but we live every day by the development of our inward man.

One of the outward manifestations of a strong inner man comes in the form of the most common way of discernment. I call it, "daily discernment."

What is "daily discernment?" It's the ability to meet someone, and from the Spirit know more about them than they know themselves. It's the ability to walk into a room and know what's happening before anyone says a word. It's knowing the difference between good and evil just by sensing the atmosphere. It's the ability to listen past a person's words and to hear what is really happening inside of them. Discernment is knowing you were sent to a person, a place, a city, or a nation, and knowing what to do once you're there.

Daily discernment can be the simplest of things, like knowing where to go and where not to go. Because of the inward witness inside you, you will know what to say and what not to say.

I'm not talking about the gift of the discerning of spirits. I'm talking about developing your discernment into everyday manifestation. You have the spiritual equipment within you that is able to overcome every situation and environment that presents itself to you.

Discernment such as this comes from your human spirit, or inward man. Your human spirit is the center of communion and communication with the Spirit of God. God doesn't speak to your brain or to your emotions. He speaks to the inner core of your being. From your inner man, you can accurately hear, know, and discern what is before you.

Daily discernment is not a mystical occurrence. On the contrary, to the born-again believer discernment should be as normal as eating or sleeping.

Daily discernment must be developed, trusted, and lived every day. You develop discernment by cultivating your relationship with God. There is no accurate discernment apart from an intimate fellowship with God. When you're intimate with God, you will trust what He shows you or tells you. It's easy to live it when you believe it.

For example, when you see someone strong in faith, it's because they've lived through some things and have tested, tried, and proved their faith. Now you see them living in the increase and strength of faith.

Daily discernment operates by the same spiritual laws. When you see someone who operates strongly in discernment, it's not an unusual gift given to a special person. It's not something for you to "ooh" and "aah" over. What you're seeing is someone who has developed the discernment equipment that we've all been given. Instead of putting that person on a pedestal, let them inspire you to begin developing what you've been given.

Daily discernment is for every believer, not just a certain group. It's part of the spiritual equipment God has given to help you walk through life. However, it must be awakened, tested, tried, and proven.

Throughout the New Testament, verse after verse tells of how believers discerned their mission by the Spirit. After the Holy

Spirit was given, these radical believers understood this was His time, or dispensation, to operate through them on the earth. They knew the priority of their lives was to be led and governed by the Holy Spirit. Everything they thought, every church they started, every business they worked in, every thought towards the government, and every family they raised were in submission to the Holy Spirit. That's why they walked in supernatural power. That's daily discernment.

Look at how Paul described the dispensation we still live in:

> **Why should not the dispensation of the Spirit [this spiritual ministry whose task it is to cause men to obtain and be governed by the Holy Spirit] be attended with much greater and more splendid glory?**
>
> 2 Corinthians 3:8 AMP

Exercising your spiritual equipment is an act of submission to the governing power of the Holy Spirit. It commands you to wake up and to stand at attention to the dispensation we are living in!

In these last days, daily discernment is part of your job.

Where's the Beef?

In this book, I've already used Paul several times as an example, and for good reason. If there was ever a man in the Bible who understood and recognized how to walk in his spiritual equipment, it was the Apostle Paul.

In Hebrews, chapter five, Paul spoke of the importance of developing your human spirit. He said:

> **For when for the time ye ought to be teachers, ye have need that one teach you again which be the first principles**

of the oracles of God; and are become such as have need of milk, and not of strong meat.

For every one that useth milk is unskilful in the word of righteousness: for he is a babe.

But strong meat belongeth to them that are of full age, even those who by reason of use have their senses exercised [trained] to discern both good and evil.

Verses 12-14

Before you can have the deeper things of God, you must first know what to do with what you've got. If you don't know how to use what you've got, God is not going to give you more. And why should He? God doesn't believe in spiritual couch potatoes. He believes in warriors and overcomers!

Did you know that many of the ministry gifts — apostles, prophets, evangelists, pastors, and teachers (see Ephesians 4:11) — would preach the deeper things of God if the people would develop themselves? Many churches are hindered in their maturity because their members fail to live in and develop what the pastor has already taught.

Many people who complain about their pastor have failed to accurately discern the real problem — themselves! Strong meat comes when the church body, on a daily basis, is operating in and living by what they've been given.

Sometimes when I go to a place to preach, I'll have another depth in my spirit that I want to minister from. But because the people have not been doing something with what they already know, the Holy Spirit will not allow me to preach it. Why? Because those people have not prepared themselves for another degree. They have not made room for a stronger, fuller meal from heaven.

That is what Paul is teaching in Hebrews, chapter five. He said, "I want to give you meat, but you can only handle milk because you've never learned how to develop your spirit and operate in daily discernment. You can't tell the good from the evil."

developing the human spirit

I've already stated that the human spirit — the inward man — is the center for communion and communication with God. It is the primary seat of our being.

As a human being, you are a triune being. That means you are a spirit, you live in a body, and you have a soul.

Some teach that we have only a body and a soul until we are born again. They say that we are only given a spirit when we are born again. But that teaching is false. From the moment you were created in your mother's womb, you were first spirit, then body and soul. Every man has come into the earth as a triune being — spirit, body, and soul.

But here's the place where the difference is made. When you became born again, the Holy Spirit *recreated* your spirit, giving you access to hear directly from God.

Since we all have a human spirit, that means anyone can operate in the spirit realm. But don't allow that to deceive you. Remember, there are two sides in the spirit realm. There is the evil, demonic power whose core is Satan, and the almighty power of the Most High God. God's power is original, accurate, and never fails. Demonic power is counterfeit and inaccurate and brings devastating results.

That's why psychics, necromancers, occultists, and some native ritualists can still demonstrate in the spirit realm. These people have a human spirit, but since they have not been born again, their spirit has not been recreated by the Holy Spirit. Thus, demon power operates through their human spirit. They are pawns to do evil, misleading work in the earth. They can't hear from God because their human spirits are unregenerate. They may show some power, but it's faulty, counterfeit, and very limited.

I've covered these points to help illustrate the privilege that you, as a believer, have been given. Upon the new birth, you have direct access to the throne of God by the blood of Jesus. What the Holy Spirit hears from the throne, He will communicate with your recreated, born-again, human spirit. From that basis, you can accurately discern the situations at hand. But you have to realize that fact, activate it, and exercise it in order to successfully operate with it.

Since God communicates with your recreated spirit, He wants you to live by your spirit. Let me state again that direction only comes from your spirit man, not the soul or the body. Galatians 5:25 states that we must live by the Spirit and walk by the Spirit to be successful and fulfill our destinies.

The strength of your spirit is determined by the degree you submit to God. Inner strength comes by feeding on and nurturing yourself in the Word of God, then following what you've read. Strength also comes from being easily yielded to prayer.

When I was a young boy, the first thing I did when I woke up in the mornings was tell the Father, Jesus, and the Holy Spirit, "Good morning!" Heaven was an intimate part of my life. My thoughts, my words, and my actions had to line up with God's or I was repenting!

I spent so much of my time fellowshipping with heaven, I could soon identify the voice of the Father from the voices of Jesus and the Holy Spirit.

God was Jehovah, my Father and my Friend. Jesus was not only the Savior of the world, but He was my Brother and my Source. And the Holy Spirit, the Great Creator, Counselor, and Warrior, was also my Companion and my Guide. I was hungry to know all of Them.

Exercise!

To begin developing your spirit man, you must also be hungry for God. You were born in this generation for a purpose, and you must desire to fulfill it. Don't look to preachers, Bible teachers, parents, or friends to do it for you. You must desire to fulfill your part in this great dispensation of the Holy Spirit.

Develop your spiritual relationship just like you'd develop a natural one. A divine and intimate relationship begins so easily. Just talk to God! Then as you go through the day, keep talking with Him and ask the questions you want answers to. When you need help, yell for it! When you need something, ask for it.

Learn to give to the relationship as well. Learn to live thankful for everything you have and everything God continues to give. Live with a heart full of praise and worship. Go through your house worshipping God and blessing heaven. If you'll do that, you'll change. You'll stay strong and focused. If you make it a part of your everyday living, you'll know God and He'll call you His friend.

Years ago I remember walking the floor saying, "God, I must have more of You. Holy Spirit, flow through me, teach me, groom me. I want all I can get and then make room for more."

How long did I do this? I still do it! Every day I walk the floor, crying out for more. Don't ever stop! It's not a one-time event. The mission of the Holy Spirit is to fill you to overflowing daily. You should be as full today as when you were first born again and spoke in other tongues. Except today, you should have more maturity, more insight, and more strength!

Understand this important point. God intends to build a habitation within your spirit man. He doesn't want to visit every now and then. In order for a habitation to be built, you must continue to hunger for both the Word and His Spirit. It's a lifestyle of study and prayer.

Hunger for God creates a purpose and a cause within you. That kind of godly purpose causes you to be swift and discerning. Remember the cause of David when he slew Goliath? His hunger for God had created spiritual strength. God inhabited David's life, and because of that David foresaw the victory!

There are times when situations or circumstances blast into your life and there's no time to stop and read the Word or pray. It's in those times that the strength of your inner man takes action and can quickly discern what to do. Why? Because you have continued to build sensitivity and strength on a daily basis. When emergencies come, you can be accurate and swift. Your spirit is the authority, not the calamity surrounding you.

When you learn to live out of your spirit, the royal nature of Almighty God will consume you. You'll walk in strength, easily yielded to the power of God.

The government of God is in the spirit realm, not the political realm. As a political king or leader is strong in his nation, you should be strong in the spiritual realm as a king and priest of God, bringing the kingdom of God everywhere you go.

A king regulates, directs, and commands. A priest heals and delivers. When you live out of your spirit as a king and a priest, your soul will serve the purpose of God and your body will bow to His plan. If you do not keep that order, you will never be able to walk in the fullness of daily discernment.

the versatile soul of man

As we've discussed, the human spirit is the primary seat of communication with God. The spirit man is where discernment originates. But in order to properly understand the strength of the human spirit, we need to also examine the world of the soul.

The soul consists of the will, emotions, intellect, imagination, and memory. All five of these areas were created by God and are a world all their own. I believe an entire book could be written on each portion of the soul. But in this segment, it's my intention to lay only some framework.

Some have labeled the soul as your enemy, but God didn't design it to be that way. He intended for the Holy Spirit, through your spirit man, to inspire and influence your will, emotions, intellect, imagination, and memory.

Just as the human spirit is the center of communication with God, the human soul is the center of communication for personality. God created your soul to be an accent, or expression, to your spirit man.

Personality Versus Character

We all have a personality, and we all give expression to it. Some of us are dramatic, while some of us are quiet. But your personality was never meant to run your life or your outlook.

If the Holy Spirit is guiding your spirit man, then He will become the very life of your personality. Under that authority, personality is turned into character.

Character is the voice and actions of spiritual laws, mandates, and principles; the voice of godly authority and governments; and the spiritual pillar that undergirds every gift and calling. Personality is simply an expression of feelings.

If you meet a person with a strong personality, you are touched or moved. But when you stand face-to-face with character, you are changed.

When a person is known by their character, their spirit and authority are usually strong. When a person is known by their personality, it usually means their soul is in command. Never mistake a strong personality for spirituality. Instead, listen for the expression of character.

"Give Me the Limelight!"

The soul is moved by what it sees, hears, feels, thinks, smells, and touches. In other words, the soul is moved by what it wants. If your soul is not ruled by the strength of your spirit, then it remains unchallenged and unharnessed.

An unharnessed soul wants to be the center of everything. If the atmosphere is not exactly what the soul wants, it becomes depressed. If the soul doesn't get what it wants, it becomes unhappy. If someone wrongs the soul, it becomes bitter. If someone hurts the soul, it becomes engulfed in self-pity. If the soul is in a hurry, it pressures everyone. If the soul doesn't like something, it becomes rude.

If the soul is rejected, it becomes obsessive or withdrawn. If something scares it, the soul worries. If someone has what it wants, the soul becomes jealous. If the soul thinks it has to please everyone, it becomes phony and deceitful.

From these examples, I'm sure you can see that the soul is not equipped for discernment. Your soul will never be able to determine your destiny. Only your spirit is equipped by God for that responsibility.

Your soul can never read spiritual atmospheres, know the hidden thoughts and plans of men, or obtain the power to heal the sick and deliver the oppressed. Only your spirit man can hear from God and determine the action to take.

When the force of human or spiritual calamity comes against the soul, it can never withstand the pressure. Only the strength of the human spirit can rise up, discern, and roar, "NO!"

Soul Has a Place

However, the soul was never meant to be destroyed or dormant. There's nothing worse than someone with a doormat mentality. God created expression! He enjoys intelligence, wit, and feelings. But He never intended for intelligence to rule over spirit, wit over character, or feelings over faith.

Don't think that your soul doesn't have a place in the kingdom of God. It does! Your soul was designed to serve God and to love Him. In Matthew 22:37, Jesus admonished a Pharisee by saying:

Thou shalt love the Lord thy God with all thy heart, and with all thy soul, and with all thy mind.

Then Third John 2 states:

Beloved, I wish above all things that thou mayest prosper and be in health, even as thy soul prospereth.

So the soul is very instrumental in the work of God, and it has its place of expression and servanthood. But you can only prosper and love God with your soul if your spirit rules. The soul is severely out of order when it steps into the place of the spirit and tries to discern.

Look Out! The Soul Is Discerning!

Discernment from the spirit is an absolute. There's peace and stability. You can look at it, label it, fix it, and go on your way. But when the soul tries to discern, it looks for the spectacular, not the supernatural.

Sometimes the supernatural is too quiet for the soul. It has to always have hype or excitement. Why? Because the soul wants to be constantly entertained. The interests of the will, emotions, intellect, imagination, and memory all want to be stimulated at the same time.

When the soul tries to take the lead in spiritual things, you can always find anxiety and suspicion. Suspicion is the voice of the soul; discernment is the voice of the spirit.

Suspicion comes from a soulish dominance in your life. It can come in several ways: One, you've been hurt and wounded in the past and you've never allowed God to heal you. Now you're suspicious of everything and everyone that even hints of your past circumstance. Or, you've heard too many opinions about something, and from those opinions you've formed a suspicion. Then sometimes immature believers go around looking too hard for evil and form suspicions from their souls instead of knowings from their spirits.

Remember this. If you're staying in fellowship with God, He'll tell you what you need to know. The Holy Spirit doesn't play games.

When people operate in suspicion, it only shows they've not given attention to their spirit man. They have not strengthened themselves by working and fellowshipping with the Holy Spirit.

I'm not writing this book to create thousands of *suspicious* people! I'm teaching you to increase and mature into absolute *knowings* from the Spirit of God. If you're going to be in true progression in your life and church, you must go from knowing to knowing; not from knowing to maybe, to possibly, and back to knowing. What a mess!

You say, "Well, Roberts, I feel this."

Well, I don't care what you feel. I'm interested in what you know! *Discernment is not a feeling!* It's a knowing. In fact, all spiritual things are knowings. Most soulish things are, "I feel," "I sense," or "I don't know."

"Well, Roberts, I do feel something. But I don't know what it is. But it's there."

Then hush until you find out what it is!

The soul tries to operate by mental work. It always tries to discern from the instability of its fear, hurt, sorrow, and emotional hope. The soul takes those fragmented pieces and attempts to turn them into an absolute.

That's why some people are lopsided, weak, and confused when it comes to discernment. They've tried to discern a spiritual situation from a soulish standpoint. One minute they think one thing; the next minute they think something else. If I've just described you, then you're either trying to discern from your soul, or you haven't developed the strength of your spirit to accurately label what you've picked up.

When you operate in spiritual discernment, you operate out of your spirit with hope, faith, and love. In fact, remember to **always** discern with an attitude of hope, faith, and love.

The Spiritual Snoop Guard

The soul operates in a critical or judgmental fashion, with an attitude of, "I've got you." Don't ever be guilty of waltzing into a place like you're the prize of heaven, saying, "I've come to discern." Just put your nose back on your face and go home!

You don't have to hunt for discernment. Spiritual discernment is *not* snooping.

There's a whole group of people out there hunting and snooping, thinking they're spiritual. They're not. They're soulish and carnal. I call them the spiritual snoop guard. They snoop and snoop until they find something. Armed with a motive to accuse, bind, and dominate, they'll even snoop into what has already been forgiven and forgotten. Then they'll use it against you!

Don't ever thinkyou can develop your discernment by hunting and snooping. That's a soulish mud pile and you may be the only one left playing. If you don't stop it, pretty soon you won't know the difference between the Spirit of God and your own soul's activity.

Snooping is not of the Holy Spirit. That kind of operation is instigated by the devil. If you've been guilty of it, repent. The devil has been having a heyday in your soul.

If the devil has sent a weirdo to snoop on you, then turn it. Don't ever let any devil or any discussion bring up the past to torment you. Whatever has been forgiven *is* forgiven. Instead, discern the snoop and call it what it is!

Remember, there are no wonderings, maybes, or snoops when you walk with God. You're not ready to speak if you just feel something but have no idea what you feel. Discern if you're being led by your spirit or by your feelings. If you're trying to discern from your own little personal preferences, then you'll be inaccurate.

If you've replaced true spiritual strength for a soulish, hound dog attitude, repent for your shallowness. Ask God to strengthen your spirit, then harness your soul so the kingdom of God can continue through you.

Come out of soulish guessing and into spiritual discernment!

practical discernment: a step-by-step developmental process

Many people ignore or disregard their daily discernment because they've not been taught how to read it and work with it. They've placed a false expectation upon it, thinking that discernment will always tell them exact names, dates, or times with explicit details. As a result, many people have discredited the discernment that operated through them because they didn't know what it was.

To help you mature in discernment, let's explore some ways it operates.

Your discernment may not always tell you what kind or how big or how many. You may not always be able to exactly label it. But you will be able to identify if it's a demon, the flesh, an attitude, a situation, or an event about to happen.

Sometimes when you're dealing in everyday situations, you may pick up something and not be able to register what it is. You just know it's there.

As I've said already, leave it there until you can label it.

Let's look again at Hebrews 5:14:

> **But strong meat belongeth to them that are of full age, even those who by reason of use have their senses exercised to discern both good and evil.**

The more you exercise your senses to discern both good and evil, the quicker you'll be in identifying a situation.

You say, "Roberts! How do I exercise my spiritual senses? When I discern something, what do I do with it?"

Unless you receive immediate discernment in a situation *and* the green light to act upon it, you need to pray about it. Just go to the Lord and say, "God, I've seen this. What should I do?" You'll find that most discernment problems can be concluded, moved, or changed by prayer.

How much time do you need to spend in prayer to make yourself strong? You have to figure that one out for yourself. Just make sure that your prayer level is overflowing every day, or you'll find yourself lacking in some area.

You have to go to the Source of Life to live a strong, discerning life. Sometimes you have to pray in your natural language and in other tongues. Other times all it takes is, "Father, am I missing it here?" and He'll let you know.

Prayer takes you into the high level where discernment and answers come. When I'm faced with a difficult situation, I call out for God and pray in strong tongues, building up my spirit man to hear His voice. That's when I receive my answer and spiritual knowings come.

At other times, the situation might not be as difficult. So I just check in by saying, "Father, what is this? Is this right?" He not only gives me the answer, but also the direction on how to handle it.

When you pick up something, one of the first things you are tempted to do is talk about it. That's your natural man, so don't give in to him. Instead, discipline yourself to pray and ask God about it. If you don't pray, you'll start talking. Weak people talk; strong people pray.

If you're new at discernment and pick up something about a person, keep quiet about it. If it's something that could harm you, keep your distance and watch. If it comes to pass and you were right, it will build strength inside of you. The next time you discern, you may have some liberty to minister to the other person involved.

Don't jump out ahead of God and speak too soon. If you do, you may get in over your head. Or, needy people might start pulling on you for discernment in areas in which you're not yet developed. Those situations put pressure on you to perform, and God's not in that.

The only time you should talk to those around you about what you have discerned is when God gives you immediate direction and it's for the benefit of all involved. Don't ever talk without direction. Even then, do so wisely.

This area is especially hard for young prophets who start seeing and discerning things. It's a natural thing for prophets to want to tell someone, because the strongest part of their anointing is in their mouths. You can usually tell how spiritually young a prophet is by how much he or she talks and tells to those who aren't involved.

Be very careful about shoulder-to-shoulder conversations. There are very few friends you can actually share with, because very few people can hold it correctly.

If you're not careful with what you tell, you may assume it's being handled correctly and it's not. Pretty soon what you asked for prayer about has become mismanaged and caused trouble for all who are involved.

If you must tell someone what you've discerned, then go to the proper leadership above you. Always go to someone who is older and wiser in the Spirit. That's how you keep developing, maturing, and going forward.

Holy Ghost Intimacy: A Part of the Process

Accurate discernment is learned gradually and it only comes by exercising it. If you've never exercised physically, you can't put this book down and run six miles. You have to build up your strength for the endurance, and you build strength by continuing to develop your physical stamina through exercise.

Developing discernment is much the same way. Take it step by step. Sometimes discernment comes with a quiet knowing. Those are the times to watch and pray to receive instruction. Then sometimes discernment comes so strong it rattles your being. Those are the times for strong intercession or immediate action. You build spiritual strength by continual maintenance.

The key for spiritual exercise is to stay tuned into the Holy Spirit and learn to fellowship with Him. The more you behold Him, the more you'll operate like Him. As you continue with Him, spiritual discernment will automatically operate. The more you exercise it, the easier it will become.

While you're learning, you may make some misjudgments. If so, then be big enough to correct yourself and say, "I'm sorry. I missed it here." If no one else is involved, then correct it within yourself and learn from the mistake.

A sure way to stop the flow of God in your life is by failing to admit an error or covering it with excuses. If you want to be fluent in discernment, you must be mature enough to carry the responsibilities of it.

making personal adjustments

It's very important to remain spiritually observant. What do I mean by *spiritually observant*? I mean to stay alert and sensitive to what God is speaking to you or showing you. Be open to His correction, adjustment, and fine-tuning in your life.

In cooperating with discernment, you must remember that fellowshipping with the Holy Spirit is not always to receive a blessing. Sometimes it means being corrected. At times it means allowing Him to cut out what shouldn't be there.

During those times, God wants to purify you and adjust your outlook. And that's where many people miss Him. They ignore the adjusting part. They want God to answer the major things, but the minor things seem insignificant.

The Holy Spirit wants to take care of the minor things while they're still minor! He knows that minor things can multiply into major strongholds. He'll nudge, poke, and point out something until you see it and deal with it.

Sometimes just an adjustment on your part will be all the discernment you need for a situation. An attitude correction may help you to see why a situation came to be or why strife began. Then you can discern what to do.

If adjustments need to be made, make them. The Holy Spirit may warn you on certain behavior, or He may give you something to say to someone that will help them.

Remember this: Some of the things you've discerned have been shown to you for your own sake. You don't need to discuss those things; just walk correctly with that knowledge. Some relationships or situations don't have to be cut off; your position in them just may need to be reworked. You might have gone too far one way and God wants to bring you back to the correct focus.

Sometimes you have to press through during your prayer times to get the peace and discernment you need, especially if you've been wronged in a hurtful manner. If your soul is bound up and entangled with bitterness or resentment, concentrate on yourself and find your release.

You'll never be able to accurately discern if your heart is filled with hurts, wounds, or revenge. An offended person never gets anywhere with anyone. They are usually the ones who crumble. An offended believer turns up bitter, critical, and looks for the worst in everyone and every situation.

In developing discernment, there's no room for finger-pointing. There is a better and higher way through the Spirit of God.

The First Finger-Pointing

I like to approach attitude adjustments this way: Everything we do comes from either a judgmental or life-giving point of view.

The book of Genesis first showed us right and wrong attitudes. Before the Fall, mankind walked in "life" attitudes. After the Fall, mankind walked in "finger-pointing." The minute Adam and Eve ate from the tree of the knowledge of good and evil, they began to blame everything but themselves for their personal failures.

Have you ever seen a Christian with a grumbling, sharp attitude, pointing a finger and saying, "I'm right"? They may be right, but where is the power and life to present that truth and cause others to follow it?

Being right with the wrong spirit is not the complete discernment package.

Evan Roberts, the great Welsh evangelist, said it this way: "You may be right, but on the wrong level." What he meant was this: If you're not living high and seeing high with the hope, faith, and love of God, it doesn't matter if you're right. If you're going to discern something and present it, then do so at the high level of God. Don't operate from the low level, which is laced with human factions and accusations.

Don't stop with half of the answer because you have wrong attitude. Make sure you're seeing the whole picture. A common mistake with discernment is that some hear in part, but they never go further to correct their own attitudes and find the answer to the problem. That's where they miss it down the road.

Learn to press on in prayer until your attitude matches the high level of God. The high level produces life. The high level exudes joy and power. That strength and joy will turn many to the right path!

Learn to live out of the strength, joy, and peace that is within your spirit. It's there waiting for you. All you have to do is tap into it and take part of it.

As you develop discernment, make sure that no soulish hardness is on you when you pray. If it is, pray until you soften and find your release. If you don't, when you start picking things up in your spirit, you'll think it's for someone else, but it's really meant for *you*!

Keep Your Own Soul "in Check"

Learning to hold your soul is simply keeping it in check and in submission to your spirit. Remember what I've already said. If your spirit is not strong and your soul is filled with hurt and insecurity, you'll start picking things up and think it's for someone else. In reality, the Lord is trying to get a personal message to you.

For instance, let's say you're in a good church where the Holy Spirit is free and the Word is strongly taught. The Spirit of God is moving and working in the room. All of a sudden you start picking something up in the spirit.

When the atmosphere is heavy with the presence of the Lord, you'll hear His voice even if your soul is disturbed by hurts and wounds.

You become aware of a fault, but because your own soul is hurting, you can't properly discern it. You think it's a message for someone in the room.

However, in this particular situation the Lord is trying to minister to you and show you what you need to personally work on. You've had trouble trying to settle it on your own, so now He's trying to help you in a conducive atmosphere.

Because you've neglected to form the right character in your soul, you've neglected to fellowship daily with the Holy Spirit, and you've neglected to study the Word, you're about to make a misjudgment. You think what you're hearing is for the congregation, but actually it's for you personally. The Holy Spirit has come to bring discernment for your life. He has come to complete you. But instead of turning it inward, you turn it outward towards the people.

So many times I've seen this happen in a service. Someone will be touched by the Holy Spirit, but because they failed to discern it accurately, the person stood before the people and said, "I feel this in the Spirit."

Well, it's *your* spirit hearing *the* Spirit for *you,* not for the people.

Discernment is not limited to a word for others or to the reading of atmospheres. Discernment is also personal. Listen to it and follow it, because it will keep you free from discouragement.

You may ask, "How can discernment keep me free from discouragement?"

There are a number of ways. We've just looked at one of them. Had this person discerned their own personal condition, he or she would not have been discouraged from giving a wrong word. When your spirit is strong and your soul is free, you can accurately discern. Then if you pick something up, you'll know it's not for you because you've already taken care of it. Your spirit is refreshed and in proper order. The knowledge of the Word is inside of you and working. Now you're free to give the word publicly because it's for the people.

Stop Comparing Yourself to Others

Discerning spiritual atmospheres also keeps you from discouragement. Once you know what you're dealing with, you can hear from the Holy Spirit and plot your course.

For example, the hindrances and strongholds in the atmosphere of Minnesota are different from the hindrances in Florida. If you're in the ministry and a fellow minister is moving at a greater pace in Florida than you seem to be in Minnesota, you could be discouraged if it weren't for discernment. What you're dealing with determines the pace. It's tougher to produce spiritual fruit in some areas than in others.

If you don't discern that, you'll end up comparing yourself to someone else. The enemy will love tormenting you with thoughts like, "You need to quit. You don't have it. No one likes you. You're a failure."

Then there is discernment for the proper season of ministry or business. I like to use examples in the ministry because it's easily understood, but this principle applies to all facets of life as well.

There are ministers on the forefront, unheard of two years ago, that today are world-renowned leaders. Why? They came into their season.

Even as you read this book, there are those still waiting, those still grooming and preparing, and those coming out into their season of ministry. But it takes discernment to recognize that we are not all on the same timetable. If you fail to see that, you'll compare yourself to someone else and be discouraged.

Discernment is a ministering facet of the Holy Spirit. When discernment is used in a personal aspect, you can know where you are with your life, where you are going, what it is going to take to get there, and the approximate time of arrival.

Discernment totally erases discouragement from your life and replaces it with peace.

developing your spiritual senses

There's another part of Hebrews 5:14 that describes discernment:

...by reason of use have their senses exercised....

We all know that our physical man has senses. We can feel or touch, see, smell, taste, and hear. The same thing is true over in the spiritual side of man. Our spirit man has those senses. The senses of the physical man recognize the natural world; the senses of the spirit man recognize the heavenly world.

Psalm 34:8 tells us to taste and see that the Lord is good. When the Bible tells you to taste of the Lord, it means to perceive, partake, and experience all that He is. It means to intimately take a portion of Himself to you and commune there.

Many times when the Spirit of the Lord moves, you can perceive a certain attribute that He has come to reveal of Himself. Flow with that, taste it, perceive it. Receive the blessings and benefits He has come to give you. I have spiritually perceived or tasted of the Lord and I'm sure you have too.

We're the most familiar with hearing in the spirit and seeing in the spirit. We're also familiar with spiritual sensitivity, which is our spirit man's ability to touch.

I would have to say that I've tasted, smelled, seen, heard, and felt the different moves and operations of the Lord. That's spiritual discernment.

Paul says that we are to use those spiritual senses to reach out and detect. Only by using or exercising those spiritual senses can they be trained for accuracy between good and evil.

Now the Liardon terminology for *reach out and detect* is what I call "putting up my antenna, using my radar, and scanning"!

I take my position as a leader very seriously. I scan my church, my staff, and I scan my Bible school students.

While I'm praying in front of them, I begin to scan the room to see if anything pops up. What I mean by "pops up" is that I'm looking for strife, division, disobedience, or willful sin. Maybe they've been someplace they shouldn't have been and something ugly got on them! Or maybe they were in a place and all of a sudden something just hit them, and they don't know what's wrong. That's where I come in.

I don't look with suspicion. I'm not snooping. I'm not hacking away at them, sure that something is there. No, I'm just scanning. If something is contrary to God, it just pops up. Then God tells me what to do. I get it off that person or out of the atmosphere. Then we all rejoice and go on. That's part of my job in watching over their souls.

When you're in a tough situation or something sounds real confusing, just sit back and put up your antenna. Then scan the situation with your spiritual radar and see if anything pops up. Many times it will be your spiritual radar that picks up the real problem underneath all the confusion.

Exercise your discernment in daily situations like that. Do like Paul says and reach out and detect.

That's what I do in my meetings. When I have the service, I'm the one responsible and accountable for what I pick up and discern. I don't do these things to control people; I discern because I have to answer to God for it. I want to make sure there's nothing there to wrongly influence the people. I want all to be well with everyone who has come.

Because I have that reputation, many people have told me they've fasted and prayed before they came to the meetings, making sure they were clean. That's great! If everyone would do that, we could really explore the depths that God had planned for those particular meetings!

You might say, "Well, Roberts, when I come to your meetings I don't want you scanning me!"

That means you've got something to hide!

That's a humorous response, but it illustrates a good point. If we are truly honest with ourselves and, above all, desire to be right with God, we will want to get rid of anything that is hindering us. When we get around a person who has discerned a problem, then we'd say, "Well, get it out! Help! Help! Help!"

If you want to continue maturing in God, you must always carry that kind of heart attitude.

Discernment or a Murdering Scalpel?

It should be the goal of every believer to have discernment operating in their everyday lives. However, some of the attitudes surrounding it have been carnal and wrong.

Remember, whether you're discerning good or evil, always approach the situation with faith, hope, and love. If not, you'll become a scalpel that cuts and divides the brethren.

For example, if you don't operate in those attributes you'll be like a young, inexperienced doctor. He knows the scalpel is to cut, but he's very misled in how to use it.

He knows there's disease somewhere in the body, so the uninformed doctor takes the scalpel and starts chopping. He doesn't know where the disease is or where all the organs are, but he'll cut through every vital thing in order to find what he's looking for.

He chops the liver to find the stomach. Then he cuts both kidneys and deflates one lung. He damages the ventricles to the heart, all in the name of searching for a disease that's in there somewhere.

That's like a Technicolor horror movie! But sadly, it happens. Instead of discerning with an attitude of faith, hope, and love, it's an operation that recklessly searches for the core problem, hacking whatever gets in its way.

Know this well: If you don't have the faith and hope for change or the love and mercy of God, then your discernment will become a murdering scalpel. It will not be the helping hand of divine surgery.

Remember, when God shows you something, you won't have to hunt. Mature yourself to operate in spiritual knowings. Make sure you keep the principles of faith, hope, and love inside of you. God will honor those who are good stewards.

chapter ten

run for your life!

You don't stand and address every problem you've discerned. Sometimes you need to run for your life!

There's the knowing of when to stand your ground, *and* the knowing of when to run in order to maintain your ground!

Years ago, everyone wanted a spiritual covering. It almost got to the point of the ridiculous. Everyone was so covered, no one could breathe!

During this time, I was asked the question, "Who is your spiritual covering?"

Before he went to be with the Lord, Dr. Lester Sumrall was the one I trusted to interact with and talk to. If I had a problem, he was the one I went to see.

I have learned that the older they are, the better and the wiser they are. The older person has something the younger person doesn't have. It's called experience.

When I replied to this particular minister that my covering was Dr. Sumrall, he said, "Oh, he's too old. You need someone more contemporary. Someone like me."

I shut down immediately. You can't talk to a fool. If you try to reason with one, you'll get into a bigger mess.

When you discern that you're in the presence of a fool, don't even try to help him. Instead, politely excuse yourself. Go to the bathroom and don't come back!

Just say, "You know, I've just thought of something I have to do." What you have to do is *leave*!

If more people had the strength to say, "I've got to go," it would save much unnecessary hassle and torment in their lives.

If you can't discern when to run, then you're in trouble.

Some people put things into your brain that take years to get out. What they've done or said may not seem to be a dominant part of your life, but it's in your memory. Then when you are under attack or you're under pressure, all of a sudden that thing flies right up to torment you. In horror, you look at it and say, "Where did this come from?"

It came from the time you didn't run!

Earlier in my life, if I had just learned to say, "Excuse me. I've just thought of something I have to do. I have to leave," I wouldn't have been lying. And I wouldn't know some of the sad things I know today!

Remember this as you develop your discernment. Know when to remain and when to run.

chapter eleven

W*herefore henceforth know we no man after the flesh...* (2 Corinthians 5:16). This verse in *The Amplified Version* reads, Consequently, from now on we estimate and regard no one from a [purely] human point of view [in terms of natural standards of value].

knowing people after the spirit

As you develop discernment, be careful that you don't disregard, cut off, or disconnect from helping someone because you don't like how they look or the natural atmosphere or surroundings. If you allow the natural to tint your view, you might not have the right discernment or the right facts about the person.

If we don't know people after the flesh, then how do we know them? We must know them by the Spirit. We must view them according to discernment.

If you've ever studied Church history, then you wouldn't be so quick to cut people off. God never looks at the natural. In *The Amplified Version* of First Samuel, chapter 16, we can read an example of how God sees by the Spirit.

In verse 1, the Lord instructed His prophet Samuel to go to the sons of Jesse. He was going to anoint the new king of Israel to rule in the place of Saul. When Samuel told Jesse why he had come, Jesse presented his oldest, strongest son Eliab. Surely the anointing was for him. But in verse 7 the Lord said to Samuel:

Look not on his appearance or at the height of his stature, for I have rejected him. For the Lord sees not as

man sees; for man looks on the outward appearance, but the Lord looks on the heart.

Before it was over, Jesse had presented seven of his sons to Samuel. But none of them were the chosen of the Lord. Finally Samuel asked, "Do you not have another son?"

Jesse replied, "The youngest is out tending the sheep."

Samuel said, "Bring him to me."

Fresh from the pasture came a young, red-headed boy still carrying his staff. When Samuel's eyes fell upon him, the Lord said, **Arise, anoint him; this is he** (v. 12 AMP).

Who was the young boy who surprised them all? It was David. He was the young boy with a cause in his heart. Not only did that cause slay Goliath, but David grew to be the greatest king Israel had ever known. Despite his mistakes, the Lord called him a man after His own heart.

We all know the story of Gideon. In Judges, chapter six, the Israelites were being ruled by the cruel hand of the Midianites. Gideon seemed as beaten down as the rest of the Israelites. When the angel of the Lord found him, he was beating wheat, trying to hide it from the enemy. Look how Gideon was addressed by the angel of the Lord:

> **The Lord is with you, you mighty man of [fearless] courage.**
>
> Judges 6:12 AMP

The angel went on to tell him that he would be the one who saved all of Israel from the Midianites. Now that's what I call seeing by the Spirit! At the time Gideon heard this, he was fearfully trying to hide and save a portion of wheat. But God said Gideon was going to save an entire nation!

There just may be another great person standing in front of you with a legitimate call and anointing. Some of the greatest ministers were those who came from the most bizarre backgrounds. That means there's hope for you!

I remember as a little boy, many great ministers came to the church I attended. I used to say, "Oh, if I could just meet them, shake their hand, or talk to them, I'd be in heaven!"

Well, I grew and the ministry grew to where I was able to meet some of them. I remember being so excited to be behind the scenes with one of these men. Several of us were together and had just sat down to eat when, suddenly, this man I admired did something I didn't like. Now it wasn't sin, and it wasn't even wrong; it just surprised me. Instantly, my admiration bubble was blown clear out of this world!

I worked on getting myself together for the rest of that luncheon. I was going through mental shock! Again, the man didn't do anything wrong. I had just had another expectation of him. Obviously, I was wrong.

Later the Lord led me to the scripture in Second Corinthians 5:16. I heard in my spirit, "Roberts, do you still think that man is anointed?"

I answered, "I never doubted that he was anointed. I think he's one of the greatest men in the world."

The Lord responded, "Then what's your problem?"

That question punched me. I knew I had a problem. The man's ministry had helped me more than any at the time. I just needed help to discern what was happening to me.

I read the verse again. Then I realized what the problem was. I had always known the man while he was operating under the anointing. I thought he'd act like that twenty-four hours a day. I never considered he was a natural man. When I saw him act like a normal human being, it short-circuited me.

You must learn how to stay hooked up with people by the Spirit of God and not allow the natural to affect you.

When it comes to this area, many people short-circuit in their discernment. Some disconnect from one another. Some have even left their churches because of it.

Here was their problem. They got close enough to the leaders or those they admired and found out those people put their shoes on like everyone else. They discovered those people had quirks, frailties, and areas they needed to work on. Their leaders were human beings, just like everyone else.

When these people saw the human side of their leaders or those they admired, they didn't know how to handle it. They had only known them as they operated in the anointing. When they saw their leaders were still human, they were shocked and disappointed.

There's not been much teaching on how to look at people by the Spirit. That's why leaders and church staff pad themselves. They're afraid the people won't follow them or respect them if they know them as human beings. Seeing people by the Spirit has been a problem, but it's one we can correct.

Grow Up and Get It Straight

There is a fact that we must all come into the revelation of: We're all human, and if we serve God we're anointed by God. When you mature enough to respect the anointing and the natural side of man, you'll walk in greater understanding.

When you get close enough to someone, you're going to see some weaknesses. We all have them. But when you get that close, you must know how to take charge of yourself.

Speak to yourself and say, "This person is still anointed. This person is still called of God. I will not disconnect from them. I will be mature and thankful for what has been imparted into my life." Then honor God in them, pray for them, support them, and bless them.

You may think that when your mission director goes home, he remains in a suit and necktie, sits in the corner, and intercedes until bedtime. Wrong!

Believe it or not, strong spiritual people take vacations. They go sightseeing and dress in casual clothes. They go to the beach and visit Disney World. Some of the single ones may even date! I'm being facetious, but I'm making a point.

Being spiritual is learning how to enjoy both the natural and the spiritual. It's realizing God has given you a natural earth to enjoy, while being surrounded by godly relationships. Becoming dead to your flesh doesn't mean life will cease to be exciting. It simply means your spirit will govern you, not your wants, desires, and emotions. Allowing Christ to live through you in the natural world is the most thrilling experience on earth!

You need to come out of that goofy "Lala Land," where everything is mystical and symbolic. Quit floating away in your own little world. Come down to where your spiritual combat boots hit the dirt. Dare to meet the needs of a lost and hurting generation. Then you'll know if what you have with God is real.

There are some unrealistic expectations that you must rid yourself of, or you'll disconnect from the ones God is going to use in the earth. If you disconnect from His human leaders, then you'll disconnect from His move and plan for this hour.

As in all dispensations, there will be many ministries coming forth in this hour, some we've never heard of before. Some will come in great boldness. If we're not spiritually sensitive in our discernment with them, we could disconnect ourselves from a divine relationship. And there may be a ministry gift within them that will help us accomplish what we're called to do.

There's another side of knowing people by the Spirit. You may have nothing in common with them in the natural. Your personality may have no connection with them at all, but in the Spirit you have a great time together!

Learn to discern that, hold onto it, and walk with it. Don't try to change a thing, or it too could cause you to disconnect from the relationship.

Adjust yourself in order to see by the Spirit of God. That's called spiritual sensitivity, or daily discernment. You'll be open to hear what the Holy Spirit has to say about your relationships and your life can stay on course.

divine progression

Dr. Lester Sumrall leaned back from the dining table and said, "I live a progressive life."

I said, "Yes, sir" — which was all I ever said if Dr. Sumrall was talking!

"You know," he went on, "a lot of my friends are old and are in their rocking chairs. They're totally in a regressive state of living, but I'm still going strong."

In the strength that Dr. Sumrall was known for, he looked at me and said, "And I want that in you."

Before I could catch the words, they jumped out of me. "Great!" I said. "Give it to me!"

He laughed and said, "Well, it doesn't quite come like that. It comes by experience with the challenges of life and how you handle demonic attacks on you. It comes by the decisions you make."

In other words, a full, progressive life comes by advancing into spiritual force and power. It comes by decisions. And those decisions are based on discernment.

It is absolutely vital that you know the character differences between good and evil. You cannot lump them all together or call evil "good" and expect to hear God.

Understand what I'm about to say. To go forward in the strength of God, you must discern the character differences between the Spirit of God, godly angels, demon power, human motivation, and spiritual mixtures.

Then, you must know how to handle what you've discerned.

Discerning the Spirit of God

Genesis 1:1 says, **In the beginning God....**

Before there was an earth, God was. The earth is His footstool, and in His presence His enemies are like dust. Creation came into existence by the words of His mouth. Then He created mankind a little lower than Himself. He delights in you and me.

In the Old Testament, or the old covenant, the Spirit of God came upon certain men and women to do His work. It only happened at special times in order to meet a special need.

We're in New Testament days, which means we operate with God under a new and better covenant. Initiating that new covenant, Jesus gave His life for every one of us to have direct access to the Spirit of God. He presented His blood to the Father as an atonement for our sins. Why? Because those sins kept us from communicating directly with Him.

Accepting Jesus Christ as your personal Savior activates the benefits of that new covenant in your life. By doing so, the Spirit of God fulfills His promise and recreates your spirit, witnessing of His presence. In Ezekiel 11:19,20 we read of the promise:

> **And I will give them one heart, and I will put a new spirit within you...That they may walk in my statutes, and keep mine ordinances, and do them: and they shall be my people, and I will be their God.**

When we are filled with the Spirit, the Spirit of God will dwell in us and do His work through us.

We can simply put it this way. Through repentance and faith, your human spirit is recreated into a new spirit. You're born again. After being baptized in the Holy Spirit with the evidence of speaking with other tongues, you receive the indwelling of the Spirit. You are now the temple of the Holy Spirit. The Teacher lives inside of you, unfolding the Word and giving you the desire for a strong spirit. You don't have to go through a religious leader to talk to God or to hear from Him. You don't have to wait for the prophet of God to come into your city and announce what God is doing. You can know for yourself.

As I've already stated, we have a spirit and God is a Spirit. **God is a Spirit: and they that worship him must worship him in spirit and in truth** (John 4:24).

When we invite His Spirit to live with our spirit, we can witness truth and power in our daily lives. Romans 8:16 says:

> **The Spirit [God's Spirit] itself [Himself] beareth witness with our spirit, that we are the children of God.**

When God gives you His Spirit, He gives you all that He is. But it can only be received as far as your faith can believe.

Another name for the Holy Spirit is the Spirit of Life. From that viewpoint, or that primary character element, we can discern the moves of God.

> **It is the spirit that quickeneth; the flesh profiteth nothing: the words that I speak unto you, they are spirit, and they are life.**
>
> **John 6:63**

This verse in *The Amplified Version* says:

It is the Spirit Who gives life [He is the Life-giver]...The words (truths) that I have been speaking to you are spirit and life.

If God is a Spirit and the words He speaks are Spirit, then you can only discern by the Spirit. *The Amplified Version* of Romans 8:14 says, **For all who are led by the Spirit of God are sons of God.**

Whether male or female, if we are led by the Spirit of God, then we are called "sons." God leads His sons by His Spirit. That's why a son of God will not be looking for a sign or a fleece. A fleece shuts off discernment by telling God, "When I see such-and-such happen in the natural, then I'll know I'm supposed to do this." That's the soulish realm. Unless you're illiterate or unable to read the Bible, an unbeliever, or ignorant of spiritual things, God won't be speaking to you by a sign or a fleece.

Some people say, "God, the first person who walks in with a pink shirt on will be the one to give me my answer." Or, "I know that my loved one is in heaven because the sun broke through the clouds and a young fawn ran across my path." If you're saying similar things, then you're being led by the natural. You don't know God in the spirit realm.

That's also why some people can never hear His voice. If you say God showed you something in the Spirit, they look at you like you're weird. No, they're weird. They're ignorant of the ways of the Spirit or they're an unbeliever led by signs and fleeces.

How God Speaks

We've discussed how God speaks through the Word, through counsel, and through the gifts of the Spirit. He also speaks through visions, dreams, and prophecy.

But there are other ways God will speak to your spirit as well. Before we discuss them, let me say this. If you want to hear from God, there are a number of ways to do it! God is so compassionate and so earnest in His desire to communicate with you. If someone misses the plan of God, that person chose to do it. If someone can't hear from God, that person doesn't want to!

The number one way God speaks to your spirit is through the *inward witness*. It can manifest as a check in your spirit or as a go-ahead sign.

The check feels like something isn't quite right. It's either not the time or the action is totally wrong. It's called a "check" because God is either wanting you to check out the situation a little more before you act or He's giving a big signal that it's wrong for you to be involved.

The go-ahead sign is like a big green light. Everything clicks into place. You feel a sense of security, joy, strength, and approval to act. Even if you don't know the outcome, it's safe to be involved if you have the go-ahead signal.

The next way the Spirit of God leads is through the *inward voice*. It's different from the inward witness. The inward voice is the voice of your spirit. Some people call it your conscience.

When the Word is strong inside of you, your spirit will rise up and speak to you. Prayer also builds certain things inside of you that your mind may not comprehend. But your spirit knows what you've built. Many time, when I don't know what to do, I pray in other tongues for the answer. After awhile, my spirit man speaks and my mind hears the answer. Then I follow it. That's called the inward voice.

The third way God speaks is through the *voice of the Holy Spirit*. Some say that He doesn't speak audibly, but the Bible says He does.

Have you ever heard that still, small voice on the inside? That's the Spirit of God speaking to your spirit. It's not voices — it's His voice filtering through your spirit. He's using your recreated spirit as a direct channel from the throne of God.

Whatever comes from the Holy Spirit will line up with the Word of God. If it's the Holy Spirit, you'll never hear anything contrary to the Word. If it's condemning or totally opposite from the character of Jesus, then it's not the Holy Spirit. Don't make a move until you've discerned what you're hearing and where it's coming from.

If you've developed your spirit by the Word and prayer, then you can be easily yielded to the voice of the Spirit. You can get so tuned in to His instructions that the Spirit's voice sounds audible. It's true that at times the Spirit of God speaks on the outside, but in a sensitive spirit, that audible voice sounds so strong on the inside that you'll think everyone heard it!

The fourth way is through *spiritual knowings*. Sometimes you just know something is going to happen or something is going to work. Have you ever known something in your spirit but didn't follow it? What happened? I can tell you. You either missed a timing or a divine connection, or you found yourself in trouble. If you sense a knowing but refuse to follow it, you'll pay for it.

Knowings are similar to the inward witness, but I personally put it in its own category because they are so strong. When your relationship is intimate with God, He comes down from heaven and clothes you in His glory. You wear it. And many times, that glory takes the form of knowings.

Some think they've got to have the proof of their knowing. But the natural proof always comes after the fact. If you've always waited for the proof, then you're usually too late. The only thing left is to learn from it.

Learn to turn that knowing into the strength to obey. Sometimes you will be able to discern the whole story. Sometimes you can only know the first episode. Faith comes by following, believing, and obeying. No matter how sharp your discernment or how intimate you are with God, He is still the God of faith. Let your intimate relationship with Him work for you. How? Trust Him and follow what you know.

How does that trust operate? It comes with the simple understanding that the spirit realm is more real than the natural. Now I'm not talking about acting goofy and thinking everything has a spiritual innuendo. *I'm saying you must trust your discernment over what you see in the natural.*

If you're in a situation, minding your own business, and something pops up in your spirit, don't be swayed by how things look in the natural. Heed the discernment. By trusting your equipment, you may be surprised at how differently things will look.

We have a tendency to think the natural world is more real than the spiritual world because we can see it. We can instantly touch the natural realm, smell it and hear it. But what you see today may not be here tomorrow. The natural world will fade away, but the spirit realm is forever.

Since the spirit realm is forever, life in the Spirit is the true reality. Once a truth is established in the spirit realm, it is solid.

The Spirit of Life

In John 10:10, Jesus describes the life He came to bring:

The thief cometh not, but for to steal, and to kill, and to destroy: I am come that they might have life, and that they might have it more abundantly.

When you discern the ways of the Spirit, always look for life. If you ever discern contrary to the vitality of life, it's not the Spirit of God.

How does that life come? It not only comes through salvation, deliverance, healing, and prosperity. That life should invade every part of your being, every part of your family, your business, your relationships, your church, and your property.

Life comes to recover what was lost, to restore what was taken, to revive what was dead, and to repair what was broken. Life comes to preserve what is right. It comes to refresh and to make strong. Life causes courage to face the challenge, then to conquer and overcome. Life causes you to regroup and run with greater insight and vision.

Many times I've been in meetings where I could literally feel the winds of God blow through the room. That's the Spirit of Life coming to impart His presence and insight. That's the time to stand and receive. Afterwards, I felt renewed and invigorated. My vision was clearer and I was totally focused on what I had to do.

One of the Hebrew words for *life* is "ruwach." According to this original translation, the Spirit of Life means to "blow, smell, perceive, enjoy, anticipate" — and here's the discernment — "make of quick understanding."[1]

No matter what situation you may be facing, the Spirit of Life will impart quick and immediate discernment. All you have to do is call for it and be easily yielded to hear it.

I like the definitions of that Hebrew word. There have been meetings where the anticipation was so high, you could almost soar on it! That's the Spirit of Life! Anticipate it! Call for it! Then receive what He has come to give you. You'll be overflowing with divine joy!

There are many old Full Gospel songs that say, "Breathe on me, Holy Spirit." What's that? It's the renewing life of the Spirit! The old-timers knew how to get what they needed. They knew how to be renewed when they were despised. They knew how to be restored when angry crowds threw rotten fruit at them. They knew how to watch a feverished baby go from the throes of death into the throngs of health. They drew upon the Spirit of Life! They knew reality was in the Spirit, not the natural. And it's from that same point of view that you must discern the will and moves of God.

Satan can offer you nothing of any permanent value. Everything connected to his realm will perish.

The Spirit of Life has come to heartily engulf your life, your mind, and your soul. It's not just a one-time event when your favorite preacher comes to town. You should call for the Spirit of Life every day for the rest of your life.

When the Spirit of Life comes into your spirit, He drives out every contrary thing. Any residue of the carnal sin nature is now in check. You can use that as a guide to discern when the

Spirit of Life is moving. If the carnal sin nature is demonstrating, the Spirit of Life is not operating.

---

[1] *Strong's Exhaustive Concordance of the Bible*, #7306. (MacDonald Publishing Company, McLean, VA)

the role of angels in discernment

Someday I will write a book on the subject of angels. But for now, let's briefly explore what angels are, what they do, and what they won't do.

First of all, the Bible is *always* your foundation for discerning which spirits are of God and which are not. It is also your basis for proper attitude and behavior towards angels. Angels are to be admired for their loyalty to God, but *never* worshipped.

Misguided Allegiance

Our generation is not the first to be carried away with an obsession for angels. In fact, one of the errors that Paul warned the Colossians of included their worship of angels. (See Colossians 2:18,19.)

When you only think of angels, when angel pictures are plastered all over your house, or when you give more credit to angels than you do to God, then you're worshipping angels.

The worship of angels comes from a New Age theology that has no idea who God is. The New Agers have wanted many to believe that Jesus Christ was the first and highest angel. To them, everything is an angel.

For example, when your relative dies, the New Agers want you to think your relative is now an angel somewhere. They teach that your dead relative, as an angel, can come and watch over you and your loved ones. From that vein, New Agers go on to participate in seances, hoping to speak to a dead loved one for direction.

From the worship and delight with angels, little cartoon cupids have been invented. If a television network wants a high rating, they'll do a segment on angels. Of course it's never accurate. They're trying to appeal to an emotional hunger that thinks the supernatural is a warm fuzzy.

Today you can go into any store and see a little clay figurine of a fat baby angel doing something cute. If it's not in figurine form, it's in a framed picture. You may even have one hanging in your house. If you want to be spiritually accurate, get rid of it.

"Cute" will never portray accurate, spiritual strength.

Angels are strong, glorious, created beings. Angels are *not* fat little babies with curly hair and tiny wings. They don't float around on clouds with a bow and arrow. They don't pout and lose their halos. And understand this, angels are not beautiful females with long, flowing hair.

Throughout the Bible, when angels appeared to mankind, they always appeared in masculine form. Although there is no gender in the spirit, all their names were masculine. The Bible *never* speaks of a female angel. Therefore, images of female angels or angels that portray themselves as females are not of God.

The Mission and Rank of Angels
and Heavenly Beings

The hosts of angels are without number. They are intelligent beings, highly skilled in verbal communication. Since the Bible records that angels rejoiced when Jesus was born and over a sinner who is saved, angels must have emotions.

The word *angel* means "messenger." In that capacity, angels are servants, warriors, and messengers representing the Living God. All created beings were made to serve and worship the Lord.

In that understanding, there are also different levels of angelic beings that carry out different orders. Just as in the natural military, there is rank and order in the heavenly host. The rank seems to be in governmental levels, similar to the rank and order here on earth.

In Jude 9, the Bible lists Michael as an *archangel*. That means he holds the highest rank of the warring angels. He is the military leader of the warring angels. Revelation 12:7 states that Michael will lead the army of angels who will overcome Satan.

Warring angels stand for the people of God and oppose the demonic evil that is trying to hinder the plan of God. There are many fierce battles fought in the spirit realm that we may never know of. If you are spiritually sensitive, there are other times you can discern the battle taking place for you and against you.

Based on Luke 1:19, Gabriel appears to be in another rank of angels — the leader of *God's special messengers.* Whenever he appears, revelation and interpretation concerning God are always made clear. He doesn't mince his words. Gabriel, along with Michael, are described in the Bible as having great strength.

The other innumerable angels in the Bible are simply *messengers.* They deliver messages and provide protection as God directs. Just as Jesus was ministered to on the Mount of Olives, angels minister to the saints in various ways. Many times when we think something fell into place and "just happened," it was really the work of angels involved in our daily lives.

There is also a rank of heavenly beings called *cherubim*. Now these are not the fat little cherubs we see on Valentine's Day. Instead, they appear to be the highest rank of heavenly beings. *They are not angels — they are heavenly beings.* The Bible never records that a cherubim was sent to deliver a message. Only angels deliver messages. Instead, the cherubim, or heavenly beings, have the high ranking position of protecting the glory of God.

Another rank of heavenly beings is called *seraphim*. Again, they were never sent to utter a word. In Isaiah 6, they protected and showed the holiness of God by hovering above and on the sides of Jehovah on His throne.

There are angels with wings and angels without wings. I have seen and heard both. Some appear as angels; some appear as human beings representing every nationality in the world.

What's the Difference Between
You and an Angel?

It's important to note that even though some angels appear as human beings, they are not flesh and blood. Nor can they ever be. In the same light, flesh and blood can never become an angel. When you die, you won't become a angel. *The Amplified Version* clearly states the difference between angels and the righteous, born-again saints of God in heaven:

> ...you have come to Mount Zion, even to the city of the living God, the heavenly Jerusalem, and to countless multitudes of angels in festal gathering,
>
> And to the church (assembly) of the Firstborn who are registered [as citizens] in heaven, and to the God Who is

Judge of all, and to the spirits of the righteous (the redeemed in heaven) who have been made perfect.

Hebrews 12:22,23 AMP

Although angels serve God just as we do, the difference is in what Jesus Christ did for us through the shedding of His blood. By receiving His atonement, He gave us the divine birthright to be called the children of God. As believers, that places us into a whole new class of being. An angel will never be called a child of God.

The subject of angels may put many people in awe, but the truth is that angels are intrigued by our relationship with God. In fact, the Bible says that angels desire to look into the redemption and working demonstration of the Spirit through our lives! (See 1 Peter 1:12.)

Although God could send angels to share the Gospel with people all over the earth, He has entrusted *us* to preach the Word to the nations. Through the power of the Holy Spirit, He has anointed us to mend the broken, bind up the wounded, heal the sick, cast out devils, and preach the news of prosperity and life in the Spirit.

We are *made* holy through the blood of Jesus, but angels were *created* as holy beings. In the beginning everything around them was good and holy. In fact, they had personal fellowship with God.

The Holy and the Unholy

With every creation of God, angels were also given a will to choose between good and evil. With that free will, some of the angels chose to rebel with Lucifer. As an attribute of his rebellion, Lucifer's name was changed to Satan.

God didn't create Satan. God created Lucifer, a once holy angel, with the ability to choose. It was his own choice that turned him into Satan.

This rebellion divided the godly, divine host of angels from the evil, corrupt group. Second Peter 2:4 states that these corrupt angels are chained in hell today.

How do you discern if aspirit is an angel from God? Here are some points to remember:

1. The number one aim of godly angels is that all honor and glory are given to God.

2. The message of an angel will always point to the Word of God and fulfill it.

3. Angels of God will *never* receive worship from you, but demons of darkness will.

4. Angels of God never come to judge you, but will give you the word of the Lord or perform it.

5. Angels of God will never add to the Word of God and give you another tablet of "holy" scripture.

6. Angels of God will never come and attempt to indwell you.

7. Angels of God will never tempt you.

8. Angels of God will help you to carry out your divine assignment from the Lord.

Now, let's discuss how to discern demon power and the unholy, evil effects they want to bring upon God's people in the earth.

discernment and demonic power

The first part of Hosea 4:6 states, My people are destroyed for lack of knowledge....

A lack of knowledge in the area of demonic influence has caused many believers to fall or fail. When we can't properly discern the schemes of the enemy, it will negatively affect our churches, our nations, and every other sphere of our lives.

A lack of discernment, or ignorance of the devil's devices, will make you immobile. *If the enemy can keep you in ignorance, then he is free to pursue and conquer you without being noticed.* If you refuse to recognize and discern the enemy and refuse to act on what you've discerned, you will become a prey to him.

Some people are ashamed or embarrassed to discuss and expose the devil. They'll shudder with excitement as they talk about psychics, ghosts, and supernatural happenings. But try to mention that the devil is behind it all, and they'll act like you came from another planet.

Why do they look at you like you're crazy? Because the devil *is* behind their psychics, ghosts, and supernatural happenings. He's keeping those people blind and entertained. If he's revealed, then psychics and ghosts would lose their mystique. Unfortunately, if those people stay in their delusion, they'll have a hard road to travel.

The Bible is not ashamed to discuss and expose the devil. And neither should we be. From Genesis to Revelation, the entire plan of the enemy unfolds. It's our job to develop ourselves through the Word, through prayer, and the leading of the Holy Spirit to undo his evil schemes.

The Warfare Preacher

I'm glad I've been dubbed a "warfare preacher." Years ago, I took all kinds of flack for my stand on spiritual warfare. In fact, there were several times when I was harshly persecuted. People who wanted help loved me, but people who liked their demons hated me.

Warfare is as pertinent to the believer as faith. Just as some ignorantly threw out the principle of faith because the Faith Movement was over, likewise some are dropping warfare because they ignorantly thought warring was a movement.

Faith was *never* a movement! *Faith is the heartbeat of Almighty God.* It always was and always will be! The truths of faith were restored during the Faith Movement, but just because God is moving on doesn't mean faith is over! No, you keep faith and you add to it.

The same is true with the devil and warfare. There was a time when the truths of warfare were being emphasized. But you don't stop fighting the devil just because God is emphasizing another truth! You must *always* keep the devil under your feet. That's a principle that will never change. You don't ever stop warring! You don't ever stop standing in faith!

We know that one part of discernment is recognizing the good. The other half of discernment is recognizing evil. It's so sad when a trauma sails out of the blue and wreaks havoc. The smoke clears, the ashes are still burning, and someone whispers, "That was the devil."

As believers, we should know before the trauma ever hits and the battle ever starts that it is the devil. We should be skilled in the spiritual war against him.

The God of Worldliness

There are times when you can easily discern characteristics of evil. For example, slander, mischief, destruction, fear, corruption, murder, lying, lawlessness, greed, rage, and jealousy are just a few to indicate the presence of evil. In the name of Jesus, turn away or rebuke those who carry those attributes. Evil has no right to come into your presence.

Second Corinthians 4:4 has been misunderstood by many people. They stop at the part of the verse that says Satan is **the god of this world,** hanging their heads in agony, pining away their days on this earth because they think Satan owns it.

But if you belong to Jesus, you're not of this world and you don't love worldly things. *Satan is the god of the people who love the world.* Read the rest of the verse! It goes on to say that Satan is the god of the people who believe not, so he keeps them blinded to the truth.

Legally Satan is an alien to this world. By default of rebellion, he was kicked out of his legal home, heaven. The Bible says in Psalm 24:1 that the earth is the Lord's and the fullness thereof. As a believer, everything He has is now given to you.

Satan and his demons are intruders and have no right to be near your presence. If he arrogantly tries to come near you, teach him a lesson through the name he fears the most — the name of Jesus. Cast him out into the void of space, clear off planet earth!

Demonic Facts

How can you discern the nature and character of demons? Remember, any manifestation contrary to the Word of God and the life of God is a devil or uncontrolled flesh. Here are just a few facts concerning demonic activity:

1. The number one purpose of demons is to hinder the purpose of God.

2. Demons can cause various illnesses and physical afflictions.

3. Demons seek to confuse by twisting the Word to conceal a lie.

4. Demons crave attention and want to be worshipped.

5. Demons cannot be in more than one place at a time.

6. Demons can hear and speak.

7. Demons do have supernatural strength, but they are not almighty.

8. Demons are the most comfortable when they have an abode — living in human beings, animals, houses, trees, etc.

Jesus taught more about the devil than He did about angels. He spoke more of hell than He did of heaven. But He didn't stop with the instruction. Jesus taught that the only way to deal with the devil is confrontation. Cast him out — discussion ended.

Since Jesus taught more about the devil than He did about angels, I'm going to discuss each of these characteristics in some detail. Why? So you'll absolutely know the source of evil from the source of God. Once you understand the basics of how he operates, you'll be better prepared to discern your enemy and take immediate action to end his evil endeavors.

1. Demons Hinder the Purpose of God

Demons are spirits who have rebelled against God. Since they have eternally made the wrong choice, they are under the leadership and direction of Satan. They hate God because He forever turned His back on them. Since they can't get to God, it is their utmost desire to destroy His creation. Their chief target is human beings. Only believers who know the power of Jesus Christ can effectively win over them.

Anything contrary to the life of God is the work of the devil. Demons seek to destroy your purpose in the earth, or to blind you from seeing it. Demons seek to sow discord in your home, your business, your church, and your nation. Once you agree with strife, you've opened the door to *every* evil work of the devil. (See James 3:16.)

Demons are also accusers. They accuse the brethren and God. Believers identify problems without accusing, because accusation is full of venom, hatred, and murder. This next statement may be hard to realize, but here it comes. Even if someone has done you wrong, there's a wrong spirit somewhere if hatred is in your heart.

We've all had to deal with someone who has wronged us. But when the problem has not been settled in the heart and it passes from generation to generation, it's the work of demons. *In short, racism, which is this kind of hatred, is of the devil.*

In Luke, chapter 9, we can read of a racial incident that happened with Jesus and the disciples. Jesus and His team were traveling to Jerusalem. They needed a place to spend the night, so they stopped in at a Samaritan hotel. When the Samaritans saw the group were Jews heading towards Jerusalem, they refused to give them a room.

Enraged by the discrimination, the disciples went to Jesus and said, **Lord, wilt thou that we command fire to come down from heaven, and consume them, even as Elias did?** (Luke 9:54).

The Bible says in verses 55 and 56 that Jesus turned and rebuked them! He answered, **Ye know not what manner of spirit ye are of. For the Son of man is not come to destroy men's lives, but to save them.**

There's the difference between the high life of God and the evil destruction of the devil. There's a higher way to handle problems, and the vengeance of the flesh is not it. You don't have time to get caught up in the darkness of someone who refuses help. You have a job to do and a mission to perform. Leave the outcome of their lives to God. You take care of what He's called *you* to do.

If demons and the devil hate God, then you are sure to be his target for accusation. Once you understand that, then you can go through the attacks without a burn. Rejoice that the enemy sees enough of God in you to hate you. Then go out and do more to destroy his evil kingdom.

On the same note, if someone wrongly accuses God of something, you can be sure the devil has come in to blind and deceive. He is an accuser. Show the person the Word, cast the devil out, and put their mind at peace!

2. Demons Can Cause Various Illnesses and Afflictions

One way Satan and demons seek to hinder or destroy the purpose of God is by causing sickness. Unless a Spirit-filled believer knows and stands on the Word of God concerning healing or operates in the gifts of healing, demons and the devil have the power to make them sick.

All through the gospels of the New Testament, Jesus cast out demonic spirits that had caused blindness, dumbness, epilepsy, leprosy, cancers, arthritis, bone diseases, etc. In those cases, demons had specifically come upon these people and caused various symptoms. I realize that some symptoms such as blindness, seizures, and some epilepsy arise from a greater physical imbalance and are not always the direct work of a demon. However, disease *is* an attack from demons on the human body.

There are various reasons why people do not receive their healing. Some break natural laws, some do not believe, some are hiding gross sin, and so on. But behind all of those reasons is still the evil work of demon spirits blinding their minds, wills, or understanding. Demons want to keep you in ignorance and isolation.

You may say, "Roberts, do you think there is a demon behind every sickness?"

Ultimately, yes. God gives life, but Satan is the intigator of sin, which brings sickness and disease. The goal of sickness and disease is to get you off the earth. Satan and his demons want your body to die so that you cannot fulfill your destiny in the kingdom of God and reach the hurting.

I want you to accurately discern the situations that present themselves to you. If the Spirit of God says, "This cancer is being caused by a demon," as a believer you have the authority to discern it, cast it out, and pray for healing.

Let me make a note here to qualify my stand. I'm *not* saying you shouldn't go to the doctor or seek medical help. If you need it, and your faith in God is that He will use the doctor as His instrument to bring your healing — then go for it! Your faith is what pleases God. But whatever decision you make regarding sickness and disease, make sure you know who's behind it. Then believe God in faith to heal you, no matter what method you choose to use.

One of the worst kinds of sickness is mental insanity.

In the late '70s, the Spirit of the Lord told me that the number one plague of the '90s would be mental insanity. That has been proven true.

The torments of society, financial deficits, hardships, persecution, and the increase of evil have caused many to go into depression, isolation, and mental collapse. Even as you read this book, nervous breakdowns and mental disorders are on the rise. In all the scientific breakthroughs, psychologists and psychiatrists are still baffled by multiple personalities.

Unlike many diseases, people usually receive or accept mental anguish because of their own soulish weaknesses. They've allowed the devil to bombard them, blind them, or deceive them from turning to God for strength and deliverance.

If you're a believer, you should walk in peace. If you find yourself out of the peace of God, you should know how to get it back and walk strongly in it. You must resist mental torment as you would any other attack of the devil. You've not been given a spirit of fear. Second Timothy 1:7 states that you've already been given a sound mind through Jesus Christ. Pray in strong tongues, meditate on the scriptures you need, keep yourself in divine relationships, and listen for the voice of the Lord in the situation.

Some mental conditions are caused by accidents or natural weaknesses within the body. But remember this: Emotional problems and demonic influence are closely intertwined. Use the discernment of God and respond as He instructs you.

You have been given power over all demons and all manner of disease. (See Luke 10:19.) Discern the situation before you. Confront the devil in the name of Jesus, cast out the spirit of infirmity, and speak to the evil life of disease to die. Then minister healing to the damage caused by the disease.

3. Demons Seek To Confuse
By Twisting the Word To Conceal a Lie

Demons like to work undercover in the shadows, through *temptations* and *wiles*.

Temptations are obvious. They are outright, blatant attacks that seem to say, "I've come to cause you to fall." But wiles are different. If demons can't get you by temptation, they'll devise a scheme and lure you into evil.

You'd be amazed by how many people misinterpret spiritual things because they never learned the difference between the character of God and the wiles of the devil.

God doesn't entice you to follow Him. What you see of Him in the Bible is what you get. He has openly revealed Himself and His character through the Word. He sets life and death before you, gives you the answer, and tells you to choose life. (See Deuteronomy 30:19.) He doesn't tempt you or trick you to see if there's sin in you. The Bible says we are tempted by our own desires, not by any lure from God. (See James 1:14.)

But Satan operates with delusions. Deception is one of the powers that Satan and his demons have, and a wile is what they use to lure you into it.

A wile is a scheme with a motive to deceive. A wile entices your interest and causes you to follow it. It always covers its true intention. Unless you are strong in the Spirit, know the Word, and are easily yielded to discernment, you could fall to a wile of the devil.

The word *wiles* is used only once in the New Testament. *But know this: Every form of deception has a wile behind it.*

In my book, *How To Survive an Attack*, I listed biblical references for deception. Each one of these deceptions was instigated by a wile. I've repeated them again in this book, because these facts will sharpen your spiritual discernment:

Those who have embraced a wile are deceived when:

They are a hearer of the Word and not a doer (James 1:22).

They think they have no sin (1 John 1:8).

They think they are something when they are nothing (Galatians 6:3).

They think they are wise with the wisdom of the world (1 Corinthians 3:18).

They have an unbridled tongue, yet they never miss church (James 1:26).

They think they can sow and not reap what they've sown (Galatians 6:7).

They think the unrighteous can inherit the kingdom of God (1 Corinthians 6:9).

They think contact and communion with sin will not have an effect on them (1 Corinthians 15:33).

They think they can lie, have no remorse for sin, and not depart from the faith (1 Timothy 4:1-3).

Whenever you see one or more of those scriptural references in operation, you can discern that a demonic wile is maneuvering.

Satan parades as an angel of light because he hates truth. He clothes himself in deception, appearing as something he isn't. If you receive the distortion and fail to discern it, you'll follow a lie.

Truth is the only antidote for deception. Truth always reveals a demon for what he is. And the only place you'll find truth is in the Word of God. Facts and truths are two different things. For example, it may be a fact that you have symptoms of disease. But the truth is that Jesus died, shed His blood, and rose again for your healing. You must learn to speak the truth and obey the truth, even if it's unpopular. Popularity doesn't keep you free, but truth will.

Demons also twist the Word by preaching their own doctrine. First Timothy 4:1 says ...**that in the latter times some shall depart from the faith, giving heed to seducing spirits, and doctrines of devils.** *The Amplified Version* of this same verse says, ...**doctrines that demons teach.**

A doctrine of the devil says homosexuality is good and homosexuals should be allowed in the ministry. Another doctrine of the devil says abortion is fine because the cells are not yet a fetus or a human being. Doctrines of devils show up in extreme feminist movements and other extreme activist groups.

A doctrine of the devil is *any doctrine contrary to Scripture*. One example is that God brings sickness on you to teach you a lesson. Or, if a woman wears makeup she'll go to hell. The New Age doctrine that we are all gods and that we all have a spirit guide is a doctrine of devils.

Psychics and other occultists perpetrate a doctrine of devils. I've been told that television psychics are beginning to twist just enough of scripture in their psychic readings to cause ignorant people to believe they operate from God.

That's not a new deception. In Acts 16, Paul dealt with same demon, the spirit of divination. The spirit of divination is behind all psychic prophecies and phenomena.

As Paul and his company were going up to prayer, a woman possessed with a spirit of divination met them in the streets. Now everyone knew Paul was a man of God. But an evil spirit through this woman had also been giving psychic prophecies to the city, and it had made her owners very wealthy.

When this demon saw that his prophecies might suffer if the people turned to Jesus, he began to put his scheme into action. So this woman followed Paul and his company, crying out for all to hear:

> These men are the servants of the most high God, which shew unto us the way of salvation.
>
> Acts 16:17

Here's a scriptural example of how the spirit of divination will tell just enough truth to lure the ignorant.

The people knew Paul was of God. This demon was hoping that if he acknowledged this fact through the woman, perhaps he could keep his following. Perhaps the people would still believe his psychic prophecies after Paul left. If he told just enough of the truth and twisted it, then he could go on concealing his true demonic nature.

But in verse 18, through the Spirit of God, Paul saw through the twist and turned it. In front of everyone and being greatly annoyed by this nuisance, he turned and confronted the spirit in her, saying, **I command thee in the name of Jesus Christ to come out of her.**

The spirit of divination was forced to leave her!

Of course her owners were furious because they could no longer make money off the ignorance of people. The spirit of divination had to leave. So the owners caught Paul and Silas, circulated lies against them, and had them beaten and thrown into jail.

But the story doesn't end there. While in jail, Paul and Silas loudly sang praises to God. God heard them and sent an earthquake to open the jail doors. When the keeper saw that the jail doors were open, he was going to kill himself. But Paul witnessed to him and that night he and his whole household were born again.

When the city rulers heard what God had done, they sent word to Paul and told him to privately leave the city. Never underestimate the actions of a governmental apostle of God!

Paul replied, "They put us in jail for all to see. Now tell them to walk us out of the city for all to see." Knowing Paul was a Roman, the rulers obliged with fear and trembling, escorting him to the city walls for all to see. Paul and Silas left in strength and honor.

God will honor those who stand for truth and confront the devil. Don't you forget it!

Doctrines of devils also show up through false prophets, false teachers, and false apostles. Jesus said you would know these by the fruits of their lives and ministries. Rarely will you see these ministries cast out devils on a one-to-one basis. You can't cast a demon out of others if several own you.

Doctrines of devils will always point to self-exaltation in one form or another. In the examples I've given, you can see that "me first" is behind them all. If you believe them, follow them, and give your life to them, you'll wake up in hell.

Religion likes to hold to doctrines of devils. Religion teaches that if you discuss the devil, it will exalt him and his evil works. The truth is, if they'd act upon the Word and expose the devil, it would probably clean their church out and they might even have to find a new pastor!

Expose the devil! Stop him cold in his tracks and refuse to give him another inch. People used to accuse me of exalting the devil because I preached about him and exposed him everywhere I went. The next time you meet a devil, ask him if Roberts Liardon ever pampered or exalted him!

Discern the wiles of the devil and rip the cloak off his lies. Stand for what is right and against what is wrong. Cast off perversion and every distortion of truth. Make every crooked path straight before you. Through the Spirit of God, be the deciding factor in the situation. In the name of Jesus, determine to bring freedom every place your foot treads!

4. Demons Crave Attention and Want To Be Worshipped

Demons have nothing going for them except what you give them. God has cut them off, so now they crave attention from you. Angels of God will shun attention and rebuke you for it. They know the focus is on God and God alone.

A demon will harass you as long as you let him. He'll torment you as long as you'll take it. He'll clamor, cause a scene, disrupt your life, distract, and pick at you until he has your attention. The only entertainment he has is using you for a pawn. Excess attention from you will get his evil adrenaline pumping.

I'm not telling you to ignore demons. I'm telling you to cast them out of your way and go on with your destiny.

I've had them come into my meetings and speak through people while I'm preaching. They seek to distract the saints from the Word and the Spirit of God.

These distractions don't get past me. I tell them to hush in Jesus' name — I'm preaching the sermon! Then when there's a prayer line, if the person hasn't left, I'll cast that thing out of them. Now they can be free and enjoy the move of God like the rest of us!

Sometimes when I'm preaching, a person will come in and wander around, moving from seat to seat. No, the person isn't trying to get a better view! Instead, they are motivated or possessed by a demon who is trying to be a distraction. I'll either command the person to sit down or, since I'm preaching, I'll turn one of my Spirit-filled ushers loose on them to cast that thing out of them. In my services, I don't give demons any room to distract and entertain.

I've heard of some people fearfully giving the devil attention, hoping he'll leave them alone. The goal of a demon is to get you so engulfed and attentive to him that you'll end up worshipping him. His purpose is for you to lose your relationship with God and focus your attention on him. And not long after that, we may be burying you.

Know this: Anytime a person worships a creature or creation more than the Creator, the person is not worshipping God. Everything you do should be in worship and right standing with God. There should be no distractions.

5. Demons Cannot Be in More Than One Place at a Time

There is one devil and many demons. Satan can be in only one place at a time. Demons are scattered throughout the earth, the second heaven, and some fallen angels are chained in hell. Remember, Satan and his demons are beings who rebelled against the Most High God. They are not equal with God *or* with a Spirit-filled believer, but they want you to think so.

Only God is omnipresent. That means the presence of the Spirit of God blankets the earth. God is in Dallas, Chicago, Singapore, England, and Africa all at the same time. He's as close as the mention of His name, and the power and discernment of His Spirit is available to you at all times, in any situation.

6. Demons Can Hear and Speak

We know demons can hear because they must leave when we cast them out. We know they speak because they spoke to Jesus. Demons also want to speak to you. As I've said before, you are the only entertainment they have.

Demons want to torment your mind until you isolate yourself or become introverted. They want you to be afraid of expressing yourself, to worry and feel intimidated, and to believe you have nothing to offer and that you are inferior.

On the other hand, the main mission of godly angels is found in Hebrews 1:14: **Are they not all ministering spirits, sent forth to minister for them who shall be heirs of salvation?** *If the mission of godly angels is to minister to the righteous, then the mission of demons is to torment the righteous.*

Demons know who has power over them, and who they can overpower. They recognize the power of the Holy Spirit in a believer. They knew Jesus and they knew Paul. But they overpowered the seven sons of Sceva. (See Acts 19:14-16.)

Demons also experience fear. They know the day is coming when they will be tormented day and night forever. That's why some demons tremble and others react violently when you cast them out. They know when they've heard words of power and authority. They know that through the blood of Jesus they are defeated, no matter how long they try to resist. Even though demons love to torment and possess, they'd rather leave and leave quickly than have to stand in the presence of a Spirit-filled, on-fire believer!

7. Demons Do Have Supernatural Strength, But They Are Not Almighty

You can never physically fight a demon. There have been times after beating him in the spirit that I wanted to physically punch him as well, but that's impossible!

Second Corinthians 10:3,4 says:

For though we walk in the flesh, we do not war after the flesh:

(For the weapons of our warfare are not carnal, but mighty through God to the pulling down of strong holds).

Make sure you discern how you're fighting the devil. Are you fighting with your natural ability in the flesh? Are you gossiping about your situation? Are you verbally abusing those who are attacking you? That's trying to fight a spiritual battle with carnal devices.

I've said this many times, but it's worth repeating. The spiritual battles pertaining to churches, divine relationships, businesses, and families are lost when the people involved go from spiritual combat into natural combat. Natural combat involves jealousies, slander, accusations, isolated behavior, and vengeance.

When we are hurt and devastated, especially if it has come through another person, we all have the natural desire to spew our disappointment upon the listening ear of another. We want them to take sides and to choose sides now!

But the wisest friends you can have are the ones who will draw a line between the carnal and the Spirit. The best friends are the ones who refuse to cross that carnal line with you. At first you may feel betrayed and indignant towards them. Just repent and go higher than the low state you're in. Recognize that these kinds of friends are the ones who will hold you to the Spirit — and that's the only way you'll win.

You must also make sure your idea of supernatural demonic strength is not one-sided. Rarely does it manifest like those wild Hollywood movies where a human being is thrown against the wall. Instead, demonic strength can rush upon your mind and encompass it like a whirlwind. Its battle design is to throw you into mental and emotional confusion.

Sometimes the strength of a demonic whirlwind is immediate, hoping to paralyze you into shock; other times the unceasing strength of it attempts to wear you down until you surrender. When a fierce battle is raging, you may feel extremely tired and drained of energy. If I've described you, then get with someone who can break the witchcraft of soulish prayers or words that have been set against you.

Sometimes well-meaning but *very* ignorant Christians send demonic activity into your life by their soulish prayers for you. *Soulish prayers stem from a personal desire over and above the desire of God.* These people misinterpret Scripture, and they wouldn't know the will of God if it showed up on a neon sign! If you're praying your personal, lustful desires to affect the life of another person, you're practicing witchcraft. If your heart wholly belongs to the Lord, you'll want what *He* wants, not what *you* want.

Here's a simple example, but there are many other varieties of soulish witchcraft. Let's say someone wants you for a mate. The person has targeted you and believes he or she is the God-given match for you. Of course, it's not God and you don't even know this person is alive. But if he or she is not properly grounded by the Word and the Spirit, he/she will pray that you'll be swayed and develop a romantic interest their way. That's witchcraft and you need to discern the effects. Understanding what is happening to you is half of the battle. Then those words must be severed from affecting your mind and body.

Demonic strength can range from devastating experiences all the way down to constant feelings of worthlessness, rejection, and intimidation. The battle is for your mind and your will, hoping you'll soon grow discouraged with God.

When the strength of this evil whirlwind comes your way, you must discern it, stand, resist, and fight back! Every demonic spirit must bow to the authority of Jesus Christ. When you are in this type of battle, bring out the biggest spiritual gun you have and blow the evil spirits off the planet!

As long as you are alive, you will face strong spiritual battles. If you don't discern what's happening to you, you'll just walk around feeling passive and drained. Every part of you — spiritual, mental, emotional, physical — will feel exhausted. You will feel like you've been beat up, because that is what's happening in the spirit realm. The devil wants to keep you in a whirlwind because he doesn't want you to pinpoint the source.

You can tell when a believer is losing to the strength of the enemy. When their spirit is weak, their mind is losing to the torment, and their body is fatigued, their voice will express it. They may say all the right things and go through all the right actions, but they've lost that punch in their voice.

I learned years ago that the strength of the spirit within a person gives off a sound through their voice. It's the sound of God. It's not a voice that merely recites a faith confession. It's not a voice filled with hope. It's a weight that thunders with the presence and assurance of Jehovah.

Develop yourself in the righteousness of God. Don't cross the line and give in to natural, carnal combat. Through sharp, spiritual discernment, you can beat the devil every time through the strength of God.

8. Demons Are the Most Comfortable When They Have an Abode

Demons primarily live in the air above the earth, or the second heaven. God lives in the third heaven, an expansion far beyond our universe. The first heaven is the atmosphere of earth.

Demons want a physical body to live in and you are their first choice.

You say, "But Brother Roberts! Can a demon possess the spirit of a believer?"

There's no room for both God and the devil. You can get so severely oppressed in body, mind, and emotions that your spirit man suffers. But don't get hung up on the letter of the law. Who cares if he's in you or on you? Cast that evil away from you no matter where he tries to come! Let the theologians argue if he's "in" or "on," but you stay free!

If a human being rejects them, they'll resort to animals. If no animals are suitable, they'll go in trees, rocks, houses, mountains, and so on.

Years ago I heard a story about a man in the Northeastern section of North America. He had gone into the fields to work and a "tree" spoke to him. After several days of this oddity, the "tree" told the man to cut off some of the bark and mount it on the wall in his bedroom. The man did it and became demon possessed.

Soon, supernatural occurrences began to happen in his home. The bark on his wall began to drip blood. Violently, he began to beat himself. In a desperate attempt to restore their sanity, his wife tore the bark off the wall. But an imprint was burned into the plaster and continued to give off an eerie glow. The violence continued.

It's recorded that while driving his car, the man began to beat himself with his own fists, resulting in a car accident. The Cardinal of the Catholic Diocese was called into the home for an exorcism. It's not known if the man was delivered. The media heard the story and exploited it on a nationwide news program. The shattered man and his family were forced to move.

Did a tree speak to this man? Of course not! A demon that lived in the tree preyed upon the ignorance of this family and took devastating advantage of them. The demon was invited in, and their lives were reduced to shambles.

I've heard Dr. Sumrall give vivid descriptions of people who worshipped trees that oozed grease and rocks covered with sacrificial trinkets. He spoke of people who had special mountains where they said evil spirits dwelt. The people were worshipping demons who lived in these material objects. Unfortunately, these people have a better understanding of demon presence than some Christians have. It seems modern man thinks he's too smart for such things.

Demons will live in houses where tragic events took place. If you live in a house that is oppressive or unusual, cast that spirit out or move!

Demons also live in prisons and jail cells where violent, demon-possessed people have stayed. They dwell in evil places, where murder and unspeakable crimes were committed.

We've said that just like our natural military, godly angels also have rank. The same is true in the demonic realm. They have principalities, powers, world rulers, and wicked spirits, all assigned to a specific area and task.

When you get to where you become spiritually sensitive in this area, you'll begin to discern the demonic powers that exist or rule over a certain city or area. Many times you can tell by reading the local newspaper. What gets the headlines day after day? What is continually happening in that city? When you trace it, you'll usually find a demon spirit behind it.

We weren't born knowing how to fight the devil. We all have to discover how, and that comes by knowing your enemy. This book is not about demons; it's about spiritual discernment. But I went into detail on these different topics so that you would have enough information and knowledge to make you disturbed. Yes, you read it right — I want you to be disturbed about the devil.

Once you know him, you should be very disturbed at his schemes. That disturbance should turn into a quest to know your authority and power. It should cause you to eagerly sharpen your discernment equipment in order to exploit him. It should produce righteous indignation whenever his evil head pops up.

The reputation I have should be the same reputation you have. It is the ministry of *every* believer to crush the head of the devil and keep him under your feet! Discern him and prevail through the blood of Jesus!

discernment and human motivation

This is an interesting topic to discuss. I've noticed people get into a lot of trouble because they can't discern the difference between true spiritual leadings and human motivations.

True spiritual leadings come from the Spirit of God. Your response to the situation is motivated by His Word and His truth. A human motivation is exactly what it sounds like. It's a response motivated by human emotion, fears, hurts, wounds, or bitterness.

You can't be led by what you see on the surface. It doesn't matter how faithful people can be to a church if they don't change their lives. It doesn't matter how many ministry positions they hold if their spirit remains weak.

Amazingly, many people are influenced by the things I've just listed. They think if a person has held a position on a ministry staff or if has done church work, that person has a strong spirit. Not necessarily so.

First of all, people are on the staff of a ministry for different reasons. Unfortunately, every ministry doesn't hold their staff personally responsible to develop their own spirit. Anyone can do church work or attend church for a variety of reasons. Many come just to see what God will do for them instead of what they can do for God. Some come just to find a date for Saturday night.

Understand that when the church doors are open, whosoever will does come in! The Spirit of the Lord then gives them the opportunity to accept or reject the change He has come to bring.

If you think whoever attends church regularly is strong in the Lord, then you are lacking in spiritual understanding. I'm sure your lack of discernment has already caused you heartache and disappointment, because it is the undiscerning who become the victims of those who operate out of human motivation.

The undiscerning are entrapped by listening to stories and feeling sorry for those who speak. Why? They listen to the story and never look to discern the root cause of the problem. They become a victim to what they've heard. What they don't know is that fifty people before them fell to the same story! So these undiscerning people are the ones who continue to pour their prayers, time, and money into a person who has no intention of changing or allowing God to deal with the root problem.

From time to time, you may have people who will come to visit with the intent of *getting immediate relief* instead of *wanting to fix* their problem. If you get caught up in human motivations and fail to discern the root problem, you'll spend a month casting devils out of your home after this person leaves!

There's another reason why some fall victim to human motivations. Sometimes the blind and undiscerning are angry at another ministry or church, so they run to help a soulish person in order to look big and spiritual. However, the only thing that looks big on them is the grudge they're carrying. Both parties need to learn a lesson.

You can't help people who won't help themselves, no matter how good you want to look.

Human motivation comes from soulish, deficient, carnally-minded people who try to keep you lassoed with their soul. They have a wound that never heals because they don't want to recover. They don't have the Jezebel spirit, which is controlling and independent, but are usually codependent people.

Here's what I call codependent: You have just enough of the Spirit to talk the talk and show up at the right places to get your handout, but you can't walk the walk. You need someone to constantly encourage and counsel you. When you don't develop a strong spirit, you will have a codependent personality.

Before we get into this codependent human motivation, let's talk a little bit about the Jezebel spirit. It's important to discern the difference between the two.

Here Comes Jezzie!

The Jezebel spirit is compared to King Ahab's wife, Queen Jezebel, in First and Second Kings. The evil spirit of Queen Jezebel affected an entire nation. Jezebel spirits have no gender, but they do appear in females more than males because of their motive to dominate without physical force.

A Jezebel spirit is strongly independent. In fact, it will not submit to anything unless it can control and dominate the situation.

People with a Jezebel spirit want you to think they're interested in you, but the whole time they're out for self-promotion. They'll put on an act of submission for however long it takes in order to get an advantage. If you yield to it, everything you've paid the price for has now become their stairstep to success.

A Jezebel spirit craves attention. A person carrying it wants to control your life and own you. A Jezebel is fiercely ambitious and will stop at nothing to gain the lead. The stronger you are or the more influence you have, the more irresistible you become to a Jezebel. That spirit is out to conquer, and the weak are no challenge. A Jezebel is out to rule the mighty. It wants to see the mighty fall.

If a female carries a Jezebel spirit, she will not live with anyone unless she can dominate and control the relationship. That's why you see some families where the husband is just a token. The wife is the decision-maker, the controller, the leader. If the man tries to take the lead, the woman will pick at him until he's shamed. If you let a Jezebel spirit control you, your destiny could be aborted.

Hear me well on this: It's important to understand that if a woman is strong, it does not mean she has a Jezebel spirit.

Some people think every strong woman is a Jezebel. If you think that, you're missing out! Don't mistake strength for evil. Strong women are not only wonderful, but they're a gift from God! You've heard the saying, "Behind every great man is a greater woman." Well, it's usually true. But notice she's standing beside him or strongly behind him, not knocking him out of the way to get the limelight!

People with true godly strength know their place and position. People with a Jezebel spirit want to take *every* place and position!

It's a Strong Woman, Not a Jezebel

In the Book of Judges, Deborah was a wife, a prophetess, and a judge in Israel. In chapter four she called for Barak, a chief in the army of Israel.

When Barak approached her, Deborah said, "Hasn't the Lord told you to go into battle? Didn't He tell you He would deliver the enemy into your hands?" Notice that she didn't want the credit; she was reminding Barak of the word of the Lord.

Barak responded that he wouldn't go into battle unless she went with him.

The prophetic word stated that God would lead Barak into victory. Deborah knew this. But if her going along was the only way Barak would go, she would agree. However, she did state that his request would go down in history — and now the victory wouldn't be his alone.

Barak did all the work and all the fighting. Deborah went along and prophetically encouraged him to follow the word of the Lord and attack. Barak did so and won the battle.

Then Deborah and Barak worshipped the Lord on behalf of all Israel. Before the people, Barak called Deborah a "mother in Israel." Notice he said "mother," not "chief independent."

A person with motherly attributes is the last person who would claim self-promotion! A strong mother is constantly giving herself for her family, praising their efforts — and jerking any slack!

Here's the difference between Deborah and Jezebel. Deborah was strong in the Lord. She didn't control Barak, dominate him, or knock him out of the way. She didn't try to take the lead or force her presence upon his weakness. She knew her place and stood strong. She didn't take the credit, but received it because of Barak's request. Her only goal was to see the word of the Lord fulfilled. She had greater courage and strength than the chief of the army!

Codependent, Human Motivation

As I've said, not every problem is a Jezebel spirit. Usually, it's just a wrong motivation out of the human spirit. These types of people have an insecurity problem and they want all of your attention. They can be harmless to your well-being *if* you know how to keep them in line.

Most of the time, these people go in and out of the Spirit. They hit it, then get wrapped up in their insecurities and stay depressed and dependent for months. They gravitate towards people who will give them handouts or take care of them without pressing them into spiritual maturity so they can take care of themselves.

They'll adopt anyone's point of view, as long as the person has the "Don't worry, I'll-take-care-of-you" attitude.

If you come in contact with this kind of person and say, "From now on, this is going to change, and this is going to change, and you're going to take care of yourself." *Whop!* Their world is crushed! You have become their number one archenemy — all because you were requiring this codependent person to grow up spiritually. They'll whine, cry, and moan, all because their soulish, emotional cushion was taken away.

Human motivation operates out of the soul with a little of the Spirit thrown in to spice it up. It operates more from logic and emotion than spiritual laws. It can look strong, but actually feels helpless in a spiritual world. It doesn't like to press in to the things of the Spirit, so it pads the soul and turns to whoever can help.

When it comes to shirking responsibility and having someone be their source of money and emotional counsel, age doesn't matter. It's pathetic to see a forty-year-old act as dependent as a twenty-year-old.

124

The real problem is this: They don't have the spiritual strength to master their soul or their body. There's always a crisis or a constant feeling of inadequacy. They live from prophecy to prophecy, hoping that a word will magically open up their destiny without them having to do anything. They keep waiting for God to do something, for a door to open, for a vision or a direction — not realizing the key is within themselves. If their spirit was mature and developed, they could retain the truths and live their lives in strength.

A person who operates from human motivation is always trying to hook up with those who have success, hoping for a breakthrough that will require minimal effort.

As I've said before, they may talk the right talk, go to the right church, and rub shoulders with the best, but it's just an act. The sad thing is, these emotional dependents are almost innocent! They are so spiritually ignorant and soulishly blinded, they barely realize it's an act! Of course they realize they don't have the strength it takes to have what they're pursuing. But instead of going after it themselves, they try to hide under the coat and ride off the success of someone stronger.

A person who operates from their human emotions wants spiritual success, but they don't want to labor in the effort. They want someone else to clear the path for them. These motives differ from those of a person with a Jezebel spirit. Jezebels will kill for the lead. Codependent people just want the ride.

One reason is because codependents don't believe in themselves. They don't trust what they hear in their spirit. Their head knowledge is stronger because they've neglected to develop their spirit man.

When a person who is led by a strong human motivation becomes disillusioned, all kinds of symptoms can appear. This person can become severely depressed, withdrawn, hopeless, and suicidal. They become seriously ill emotionally, mentally, or physically; experience disorders such as overeating or undereating; or become involved in substance abuse.

Yet they've appeared to be spiritual — so you misread the real problem and think they have a devil. You go over to their house and start casting something out that's not going to budge. Why? Because the person is wrapped up in a soulish human motivation — a weak spirit — and until that is remedied, they are going to be dependent on anyone who will support them.

How To Help

Remember, people who live out of their human motivation are looking for happiness without much cost. They will latch onto whoever or whatever they think can provide that source of happiness. Then they can feel threatened by the loss of anything or any person who has provided that happiness.

Discern the motive and address it in the spirit. Don't think you're being spiritual if you continue to give handouts or be an emotional security to the codependent.

Any time you operate from or respond to an emotional need instead of a divine command, there will be no fruit. The soul can give no lasting reward. The deed you gave in to will be your only reward.

Govern your words and commitments. Do only what God has told you to do. Don't ever feel obligated under soulish requests.

You say, "But Roberts, can't I identify with their hurts?"

You can identify with the hurt, the loss, and the feelings. But that's all your soulish emotions can do except cause confusion. Many times people want to hear your emotions instead of your spiritual commitment to victory. They'll try to draw you into the emotional realm of it, and before you know it, you're in the problem with them! By the time you get that far, your spiritual, ministerial, and discernment efforts are very low. Why? Because you've identified too much with the problem and can't see clearly either.

You can support something in the spirit without getting your emotions involved. You may ask, "But Roberts, don't you feel sorry for them?"

Of course you feel sorry for them. But you don't live, operate, and direct your destiny — or the destinies of others — by the pain you feel. We live by the Word and the Spirit.

Convenience

If left unchecked, human motivations try to creep in on everyone. For example, sometimes people temporarily live or relocate to a lonely region of the world. They've left their friends and family back home. There are no social activities, nothing that this person is familiar with in this new region.

Suddenly, this person begins to talk with someone. He wakes up some morning and finds himself in love.

No, he hasn't found love. He's found convenience.

He was lonely so he gave in to his soulish emotions for relief. While he's in this region, he won't see his mistake. But after he's out of that territory and back into the familiar place where he plans to live, he'll find out that a mistake was made! And unfortunately for some, there were too many commitments made to change it.

Because of convenience, some people get so far into a situation that they can't see their way out of it. Or sometimes the way out is filled with so much misery and pain that they think, "What's the use?" So another life is set on the path of heartache because of emotions and a weak human spirit.

What should you do? Well, there's a thing called the telephone. Pick it up and call someone! Airlines offer cheap rates. Buy a ticket and go somewhere — see your friends, visit your family, go see Mickey Mouse. At that time, your life is like the commercial: It's time to reach out and touch someone!

Here's where you must discern the real facts. The conduct of your life has much to do with the fulfillment of your call. It's far better to believe God for money to travel than to spend the rest of your life in a deficiency because of convenience.

Humans and Goofiness

Now there are also human motivations that manifest as the flesh. In that case, you have to discern what is the Spirit of God and what is human flesh.

For example, in a certain city there is a move of God that is known throughout most of the world. I'm for this move of God and I believe it's a refreshing from heaven. However, there's also a lot of flesh in these meetings.

I'm not being critical. You should know that before a truth is ever presented, all sides must be analyzed in comparison to the character of God and the Word of God.

In any spiritual refreshing, there is no such thing as perfection. There is no such thing as a perfect church, a perfect Bible school, a perfect pastor, and so on. Here on earth, it does not exist.

The move of God began from heaven and came to the earth as perfect — but it came through imperfect vessels. We are the ones who give a twist and a taint to it. We may not intend to, but sometimes we do.

For example, in this particular move I've mentioned, God came to visit them in a wonderful way. He came and brought a beautiful outpouring of His presence. He spoke with them, healed them, and delivered them.

Of course, word of this outpouring spread throughout the world. Now you can see people in those services "shooting buzzards flying through the room." What does that mean? They're taking their finger, pointing it like a gun, and boom! boom! — they are supposedly shooting invisible buzzards flying through the room. We have adults, in the name of God, shooting buzzards no one sees.

Give me a verse in the Bible on that.

You might ask, "Is that a devil?"

No, it's just uncontrolled, ignorant flesh. It was motivated by an overactive human motivation. Someone in leadership should tell these people that you don't shoot buzzards, you bind them up and cast them out!

You're going to see all kinds of things when the move of God hits an area. *But many times it's the lack of discernment in the leadership that hurts the pure moves of God.* This kind of leadership allows the flesh to have free reign with the Spirit, and eventually the Spirit is quenched.

You've also got people in this city down on all fours, acting like animals. They say they're roaring like a lion. Where's that in Scripture? In the Book of Isaiah, it does say that the Spirit of God roars — but not on all fours!

I believe in the roar of God. I've heard that roar and the authority that came out of it. I've heard it mainly in corporate church meetings when an incredible anointing of supernatural strength came down from heaven and the people responded with a shout. It sounded like a holy roar! In fact, it was monitored on the Richter scale and measured louder than the starting jets of an airplane! That, my friends, is supernatural. I believe those kinds of atmospheres are the only places where these types of scriptures can manifest.

No place in the Bible will you find where God wants you to act like an animal. The Holy Spirit wants you to live and act like Jesus, not like some lion in Africa. Instead, He's been trying to get you to come out of that animalistic, carnal state of mind. He's trying to get you to live high — not on all fours. The only people in the Bible who lived on all fours had been cursed. They were delivered only as they repented.

You say, "But Roberts, the Spirit of God came on me to roar."

No, He probably came on you, but you decided to react to that anointing with your flesh. So you roared.

You can take certain willful directions with anointings. Under the anointing, your flesh can still do what it wants to do if you let it. But you will abort the intent of the Spirit of God. You are so busy fleshing out, you don't get what He came to give.

So you ask, "Well, are moves of God like this one of the devil?"

No! But you must deal with the flesh in these moves, or deal with the consequences of passive leadership. Passive leadership will cause a move of God to end, just like the story of Seymour and Azusa. I'm going to talk about Azusa in the next chapter. But understand that in dealing with the flesh, you don't have to be hard or mean. Just teach and train so the people can get the full benefit of the anointing.

The flesh is the number one way to disqualify yourself from the world of discernment. If you are in constant contact with someone who operates from a weak spirit, then deal with them in truth. Reveal to the person where they're robbing themselves and encourage them to develop their inner man. Discern which direction you should take in your counsel with them. If they refuse to change their lives, then love them from a distance and pray for them.

discernment and spiritual mixtures

And they shall teach my people the difference between the holy and profane, and cause them to discern between the unclean and the clean.

Ezekiel 44:23

Mixtures blend good and evil — and then call it holy. They mix brass with gold and call it pure. Mixtures are a meeting where the flesh, demons, and a little of the Spirit manifest and people call it revival.

Webster's New World Dictionary defines *profane* as "showing disrespect or contempt for sacred things; to treat (sacred things) with irreverence or contempt."[1]

Mixtures are a profane stench in the nostrils of God, because they recognize no spiritual absolutes.

On the streets and in the church, people seem to be confused about what to stand for and what to stand against. It seems individual conscience has replaced the Word of God. In other words, if a person's actions go against the Word of God, but feel right in the particular circumstance, then the person thinks it's okay. Wrong!

That same attitude has crept into the Church. There has been the mixing of the holy with the profane, the clean with the unclean, and the true with the false. Some of the Church has been committing spiritual adultery with both the world and psychic, New Age doctrines. Some call themselves Christians, yet plan their daily activities from their horoscope and their futures with a psychic. And once that false seed gets inside of you, it will produce evil mixtures in your outlook and understanding. It will be very hard to see the truth, much less to stand for truth, because your seed has been mixed. You've been involved in spiritual adultery.

It seems this generation is obsessed and delighted with lies and gossip, so it has seared its conscience from recognizing a stand with truth. It'll laugh at one thing, then run to learn from it. People have thrown away common sense at the price of being entertained.

Mixtures think there are many roads to heaven. In fact, New Agers are calling true believers the "antichrist" because we believe Jesus is the only way to heaven. New Agers say that it's obvious there are many ways to God. They think it's intellectually and spiritually superior to believe in many gods, but isolating and illiterate to believe in only one God. In other words, more is better.

To New Agers, embracing the belief in many roads shows what an open, educated person you are. They give validity to everyone's "spiritual" experience and open themselves to "walk-in's" — spirits or spirit guides who walk in and invade their person. They romance whatever brings them peace — no matter how temporary that peace may be.

Then there are Christians who think that barking like a dog or howling like an animal is perfectly acceptable in a church service. Those people think any kind of supernatural manifestation is acceptable with the Holy Spirit.

My friend, this is not a new way of operating in the things of God. This is directly linked to the old Gnostic belief that the world is evil so *anything* spiritual is good and acceptable. The Gnostics accepted visions, prophecies, and spiritual experiences without restraint. They had no discernment towards the true character of God. They thought anything spiritual was good.

Here's another example of mixtures. It's called "user friendly" churches, but there's nothing friendly about them. They base their strength on an ability to attract a certain demographic age group or adapt their structure to draw families with a certain financial status. They see their ministry as big business and resort to the world's system to keep the finances flowing. Know this: Clout and compassion do not easily mix.

Gold or Quick Fixes?

The Bible gives several stories pertaining to mixtures. One is found in First Kings, chapter 6. Solomon and the people wanted to build a temple for God.

Solomon came from a godly heritage. He had learned how to pay the price. At the time he built the temple, Solomon knew the standard of God and taught it to the people.

The people of Israel honored God and kept His presence first in their lives. They stopped at nothing to give Him their best. The Bible says that as the people built His temple, they overlaid it in pure gold. In fact, throughout the chapter it's repeatedly stated that the temple was overlaid with gold. That's quite a feat considering that once the Israelites were hiding wheat from their enemies in order to eat!

But in Second Chronicles, chapter 12, we read that the standard was lowered. A different ruler, King Rehoboam, was now king of Israel. He didn't care to sacrifice to the Lord, because the relationship wasn't number one in his life. He just wanted to be well-liked and popular with the Israelites *and* with their enemies.

King Rehoboam forsook the laws of his godly heritage and became unfaithful to the Lord. Therefore, God removed His hand and their enemies came down upon them. Shishak, king of Egypt, was about to conquer Israel.

Even then God gave Rehoboam another chance. He sent a prophet to him and the king repented. The Lord decided to spare Rehoboam and Israel from being totally conquered, but Shishak stole the gold from the temple and took it home to Egypt.

What did Rehoboam do? He replaced the gold with brass.

Did you get that? He wanted a quick fix. He didn't want to take the time to purify himself and the people. He didn't want to sacrifice any more than was necessary. He wanted something that looked as good as gold, without the price.

It was still the temple that was made for the presence of God, but now it was overlaid in brass.

In his feeble understanding, Rehoboam probably felt sorry for himself. He probably thought that God would understand since the gold was stolen. But the gold was stolen because Rehoboam opened the nation to sin!

Dr. Sumrall said that when a minister gets out of line and makes a mistake with gross sin, that minister has to temporarily drop out of the race until he can get it right. Time and time again, he saw a minister get it right and then want to pick right up where he left off.

But he can't.

He has to go to the back of the line and start again. He has to regroup, plow the same territory, and pay the same price. Over and over Dr. Sumrall would hear these ministers say, "It's not like it was."

No, the person has to start all over. Many of them would quit or just do whatever they could get by with. Today, you don't even know who many of them are.

That's what Rehoboam did. He put the brass in place of the gold — it was still shiny metal. But he didn't regroup to start over and pay the price or plow the spiritual atmosphere so they could bring in the gold. Instead, he settled for brass. Rehoboam just did what he could get by with.

God didn't allow the enemy (Egypt) to conquer Israel, but the enemy dwelt among them. As a result, Israel was filled with spiritual mixtures. Historically, Rehoboam is remembered as an evil and weak leader.

The Church of Absolutes

Today, some build spectacular buildings and spare no expense. Then they preach a lame gospel based on the latest Gallup poll. They think if they act exuberant, God will count it as a spiritual, life-changing sermon.

In reality, they're afraid they'll lose people if they preach the true Gospel. They're concerned the world will not feel comfortable coming to their church if they preach like Jesus did. So they preach a message everyone would like — Christians, Buddhists, New Agers, Scientologist, and whatever else.

Everyone comes to their church but Jesus.

It's a perfect time for the clear-cut, absolute voice of the Lord! If you have to take someone's head and physically turn it towards life, then do it! If you have to make every crooked path straight, then step in and take over.

The turn-of-the-century church must be a church of absolutes. You must know how to stand for the right and against the wrong. That is the strength that sharpens the cutting edge. *The cutting edge divides between the good and the evil, clearly giving you room to choose your side.* There are no mixtures or gray areas with the cutting-edge mentality.

One thing the cutting-edge church will do is take its place in spiritual government. It won't sit in an isolated world, thinking the natural government will handle all their problems!

While I do not believe in the secular definition of the separation of Church and state, I do believe we have different roles as Church and state. *Separation* and *different roles* do not have the same meaning. We can have different roles and still support one another. In fact, that's how Jesus patterned the Church to function, each with our different callings and giftings, each motivated for one goal.

To me, "separation" means to disconnect or part from something. "Different" means something has a distinct role or function in the overall picture.

The Constitution of the United States has never stated that a person in government could not express or openly practice his or her religious belief. But in the 1960s the atheist, Madelyn O'Hare, campaigned for her warped interpretation of the Constitution and won. As a nation, we've been forced to follow that interpretation ever since.

It was never the intention of Jesus to overtake the natural government and force it to serve Him. If it had been, He would have taken both the heavenly and earthly rule in His lifetime. After all, the Jews were looking for a great earthly king.

Instead, He proclaimed that His people would be a chosen generation and a peculiar people. His is a spiritual government. This spiritual government, which was on His shoulders, has now been passed onto our shoulders.

The Church is anointed to do what the natural government cannot do. We've been given the spiritual capacity to feed the hungry, take care of the poor, heal the brokenhearted, and show the way of liberty to the captives. The natural government is given to regulate and supervise the areas for which the church is not responsible.

There can be no more mixtures. We must know what we're about, what we're for, and what we're against. No more sitting in a corner and pointing a finger at the government — we have been forcing the government to do our job!

The natural government can't go into the inner city and say, "Love your neighbor as yourself," and expect all the problems to be solved. No, that's the job of the Church.

It's our job to express the Word of God and the laws of the Spirit by teaching them, praying them, and living them. The natural government is only equipped to handle surface problems such as gun laws, zoning, and day-to-day maintenance. But it is the spiritual governors and leaders who will go into regions and bring the heavens under the rule of God. The people of those cities will be free to grow in the wisdom, discernment, and purity of God. Spiritual governors can reveal where mixtures have deceived the multitudes. It is their job to disarm perverted wisdom.

Mixtures must leave before you can receive certain things from heaven.

In Exodus 30:9, Moses commanded that Aaron be the only person to offer the incense of fire to the Lord. It was meant to be a source of purity, continual praise and worship towards heaven. But in Leviticus 10:1, we find that Aaron's two sons, Nadab and Abihu, took it upon themselves to offer fire unto the Lord.

The Bible says that the Lord called it "strange fire."

Anything that doesn't think like God, act like God, or talk like God, He calls "strange." So the world thinks you're weird for following God and believing Him? No, God says *they're* weird. If you are contrary to God, you are strange!

When I was a teenager, I wanted to be with God all the time. I didn't act like the other guys at our school. It's not that they did wrong; it was just that our interests were very different.

One day the guys came to me and said, "Roberts, what's wrong with you? Why do you want to read about God all the time and study? You're weird!"

I replied, "I know I'm weird, but I'm not changing!"

Afterwards the Lord rebuked me. He said, "Roberts, quit agreeing with a lie."

I thought, *A lie?*

He answered, "Yes. A lie. Those who don't do what I ask them to do, *they* are the weird ones!"

Nadab and Abihu got something they weren't ready for. In response to their strange fire, another fire from heaven came down and devoured them. They died.

I believe the definition of their names describes the two ways the fire of God will come to consume. We all know how the Old Testament can give many physical examples of a spiritual principle in the New Testament.

Nadab in Hebrew means *"liberal."*[2] *Abihu* in Hebrew means *"father, worshipper of God."*[3]

When you lower your God-given standards and choose to abandon what you've known in the Word, you open yourself up to apostasy and deception. The walls of strength you've built through the Word are broken down. Liberal, carnal thought patterns or evil beliefs are allowed entrance.

Suddenly, you think it's no longer sin to have sex with your date. It's okay to commit adultery — as long as you still really love your mate. It's not a problem for you to denounce authority, especially if they disagree with you. It's okay to go to a seance or call a psychic, because it's all in fun. It's wrong to kill animals, but it's okay to have an abortion. You support Gay Rights because you have a warped definition for brotherly love.

You've become *liberal.*

Mixing your fleshly lusts with the things of God will cause you to sizzle when the fire of God comes. We are living in the days when the fire of God is coming upon the Church. We sing a song called "Blood and Fire" that expresses a yearning for the fire of His Spirit to consume us. But as we worship and make offering to the Lord, we must make sure our offering is not a strange one.

Make sure you've not mixed in unfaithfulness, rebellion, or apostasy when you stand to receive. God doesn't mix His holy fire with a strange, evil one. Just like the rod of Moses became a serpent and devoured the serpents of the Egyptian magicians, we are coming to the days when the fire of God will either fulfill or kill a work because of mixtures.

That is why many places can't carry the strong glory of God. There's too much garbage going on, too many mixtures in the people's lives. If the glory of God came down too thick and too strong, judgment would hit.

But just as *Abihu* means "worshipper of God," it also shows us that the fire of God can also cleanse us from sin. If you've got things in your life you want to be free from, then bring them to Him and allow His fire to consume them. That holy fire can burn out demonic influences and kill the thought patterns that have kept you bound.

It all has to do with the desire of your heart. If you try to keep your sin and mock the presence of God, you could die clutching that sin. But in humble repentance, if you present your sin for Him to consume, you'll be cleansed by His holy fire.

Why the Persecution?

Some of your greatest persecutors are the ones who walk in mixtures. That mixture in them does not want to be separated. If you walk strongly in absolutes, then your spiritual purity is challenging their mixtures and they don't like it.

Mixtures are another reason why many people can't be a part of what God is doing. Mixtures cause impurities in your life and in your thought patterns. With every new level in God, there will come a new cleansing. If you refuse to allow His Spirit to rid you of what is holding you back, you'll not move on with Him. You'll stay right where you are.

The most joyful people in the world are the people who walk in strength and absolutes. Mixtures cause sadness, depression, and frustration. It's a constant war of wrong against right, darkness against light. If you think you're doing all the right things but still are plagued with sadness, check your life. Are there any mixtures or beliefs you've accepted that are contrary to the purity of the Word? Change your lifestyle and the joy of God will return to you.

That's why many people are opposing the true moves of God and refuse to take part in it. Actually, they're unable to take part until they allow God to cleanse them. They've refused to let go of their mixtures — gossip, slander, loose morals, unteachableness, traditions, lying, jealousies, etc. — so they can't experience what others are receiving. Some of these people still go to church; they've just removed themselves from active participation. When the fire of God comes on the scene, they withdraw because they want to hold onto what they like. Instead of letting go of their sin, they bite at you!

Mixtures and Transitions

That's also why it's hard for some people to make transitions from one move of God to another. History has shown that people have a hard time living in revival for long periods of time. At first, everyone is hungry for God and eager to clean up their lives just to experience Him. But after they get used to His presence, they begin to get comfortable. That's when mixtures, traditions, and preferences creep in. The people of the revival begin to relax their standard. They get set in their system and resort to entertainment in order to keep a crowd.

When you find yourself getting comfortable, push yourself — pay the price to go to the next level. Pray, fast, and seek direction through the Word. You'll receive another divine challenge to meet and conquer. That's how to keep the true momentum of God going strong. Don't settle for anything less.

Comfortable services and predictable meetings soon bring spiritual error. The great Azusa Street Mission revival was one example.

Azusa is a popular revival story and I, along with countless others, applaud their efforts. In my book, *God's Generals: Why They Succeeded and Why Some Failed,* I tell the story of the Azusa Street Mission. The revival started like a whirlwind and spread throughout the nations like a wildfire. Azusa was the catalyst for the international Pentecostal experience.

But the death of Azusa was as dramatic as its birth. We'd better learn what caused the death of revival and prevent it from happening through us.

If you study Church history, you'll find the leadership was one of the main problems of Azusa. Seymour was a very good man. He was well-liked and the Spirit of God manifested through him. But he had one weakness that caused him to fail. Seymour was not a man who would confront or deal with the flesh. Although the Spirit would manifest through him, Seymour didn't know how to *lead* by the Spirit.

I've read all the letters Seymour wrote, studied his doctrine and his style of ministry. I've come to the conclusion that there were three things that caused this weakness. First, he was a black man who was a very popular leader during the days of the Jim Crow Laws. It could have possibly hindered his ability, even though he was in California.

Secondly, in those days it was thought that if you touched a move of God, you'd lose it.

Well, it's all based on *how* you touch it and *what* you touch that's important. You don't touch God! Some people go straight to Him and tell Him no.

You leave God alone and touch yourself. Get your flesh in line with what He's doing and cast devils out, but you leave God's part alone. If you do that, He'll anoint you and show you how to teach the people to get more from the anointing. That's how you go from one level to the next. You have to know how and what to touch.

Thirdly, Seymour didn't test the spirits. If someone fell with a demon, they thought the Holy Spirit would cast it out Himself. The Bible tells *believers* to cast out devils. They had so many new manifestations, they weren't sure what was God, what was the flesh, or what was the devil — unless it bit them.

All sorts of fleshly and demonic mixtures began to creep into the Azusa revival. Witchcraft, false doctrines, legalism, and sin began to run rampant throughout the mission. Even ministry staff members held to strong false doctrines and legalisms. Soon those mixtures began to weaken the hunger of the people. Conflict developed within the local church body.

I don't think spiritual discernment was ever a part of the Azusa revival. They had an outpouring of the Holy Spirit, but they never understood how to work with it, judge themselves by it, or cleanse their lives of fleshly attitudes.

In only three and a half years, the great Azusa Street Revival was dead. And without spiritual discernment in operation, those three and a half years were by the grace and mercy of God.

As I've stated before, I discuss in detail the dramatic beginning and ending of Azusa in *God's Generals: Why They Succeeded and Why Some Failed*. But in this book, I want to state that in order to keep your discernment alive, you must pay the price for every new level of revival.

Every wave hits the beach and comes to an end, but every surfer picks that board up and runs back out into the water to meet the next wave. You don't see a single surfer sitting on the beach, crying or comfortable because his wave came to an end.

There are surfers who have more sense than some Christians.

The Antidote

In a move of God, never take the attitude of "whatever happens will just happen." Yes, God has freedom. No, the devil doesn't. Barking like an animal is not freedom, my friend. A person with discernment needs to put a collar on and cast that devil out!

With every new mixture that tries to creep in, you must meet it with the spiritual strength of present truth.

God is truth, and He is a God of the now. There is truth and there is *present* truth. Every situation that happens to us is a *present* situation. Therefore, it calls for a *present* truth.

Present truth always comes in the form of absolutes. There is no weakening. There are no mixtures. Present truth cuts and divides because it discerns accurately.

For example, the '80s mentality cannot hold the anointing of the '90s. Even though the truths of the '80s go with us, you cannot have spiritual success unless you come up to the standard and operation of the '90s anointing.

What is the antidote for mixtures? Spiritual hunger and present truth. Don't ever lose your hunger for God! It's that hunger that causes your desire for God to be greater than your desire for sin.

As you fellowship with Him, He'll tell you where you've been weak. Daily discernment activates present truth. And once that revealing, present truth comes, it produces a cutting edge that separates every evil mixture.

Live like you know who God is. Quit living and acting like the world. Don't be frustrated and discouraged as one with no hope. Do what you're supposed to be doing and do it strong.

Fulfill the destiny God has for you, with no apologies and no shame!

---

[1] *Webster's New World Dictionary.* (Webster's New World Dictionaries; Cleveland, OH, 1990)
[2] *Strong's Exhaustive Concordance of the Bible,* #5070. (MacDonald's Publishing Company; McLean, VA)
[3] Ibid., #31.

sharpening your discernment

It takes several aspects to form a whole picture of accurate discernment. In previous chapters I've discussed the daily experiences of discernment and have gone into great detail on the character understanding between good and evil.

The next aspect I want to discuss is the development of spiritual character within *yourself!* If you overlook what I'm about to show you, your discernment will be dim and incomplete. In the Roberts Liardon translation of 2 Peter 1:1-9, the Bible says that if your character is underdeveloped, you will be spiritually blind.

One of the greatest chapters in the Bible on curing spiritual blindness is found in Second Peter 1:1-9. I like to refer to it as a spiritual character manual, telling us how to keep our spiritual equipment sharp and accurate.

> **Simon Peter, a servant and an apostle of Jesus Christ, to them that have obtained like precious faith with us through the righteousness of God and our Saviour Jesus Christ:**
>
> **Grace and peace be multiplied unto you through the knowledge of God, and of Jesus our Lord.**
>
> Verses 1,2

In *The Amplified Version*, verse 2 describes *peace* as **perfect well-being, all necessary good, all spiritual prosperity, and freedom from fears and agitating passions and moral conflicts.**

How does a person walk in that kind of peace? The Bible tells us. Through the ...**knowledge of God and of Jesus our Lord** (v. 2 AMP).

We gain a great and wonderful abundant life through Word knowledge. I'm not talking about confessing certain scriptures in order to get wealth or to seek a gift. I'm talking about eating and inhaling the Word of God for our own daily well-being. The Word gives life and light. When we study the Word in order to know God, then we will meditate on what we've learned and view life accordingly.

No matter what tries to happen in your life, there is knowledge for handling it in the Word of God.

According as his divine power hath given unto us all things that pertain unto life and godliness, through the knowledge of him that hath called us to glory and virtue:

Whereby are given unto us exceeding great and precious promises: that by these ye might be partakers of the divine nature, having escaped the corruption that is in the world through lust.

Verses 3,4

God has already given you His divine power and His spiritual equipment. And with that power and equipment, He has given you precious and exceedingly great promises.

Did you know the Bible is the only book in the world that is alive? The Word of God is the only book of promises that, if believed and acted upon, will produce life.

Scientists are always trying to mislead the nations by saying they're coming close to locating the end of the universe. What a lie! The universe came into being by the spoken Word of God!

That Word is still producing today. Somewhere in the vast limits of the farthest universe, you could still hear the voice of God command, "Light, be!" And wham! The universe continues on.

When the Word of God fills your being and becomes alive through you, the spoken Word of God will produce!

When we understanding the power of the known and spoken Word of God, we understand it is through these promises that we have our deliverance and escape from evil! His Word says we can escape all the moral decay, lust, greed, and corruption that's in this world. By knowing and receiving these promises, we will become partakers of His divine nature.

Making sure we have first things first, Peter goes on to give us a blueprint for discernment:

And beside this, giving all diligence, add to your faith virtue; and to virtue knowledge (v. 5).

Peter didn't say to give your average attention to what he's about to say. He said to give *all* diligence — all your careful attention, perseverance, and unrelenting hard work. What he's about to say involves personal responsibility on your part. You have to develop it through continuance and endurance. It's a continual lesson in Spirit life. It's never over and you never arrive to know it all. There's always more. There will always be the exciting challenge of hearing, understanding, and applying what you've learned.

You can't get it from Roberts Liardon. It won't come from your favorite preacher or prophet. Your pet campmeeting won't give it to you, nor will your favorite Christian television station. If you want it, you have to get it yourself.

Peter begins the spiritual blueprint by telling us that faith is the foundation or pipeline through which the blessings of God will come. Understand that faith is not the thing that fetches and brings blessings. If you think that way, then you're taking the credit for all the things you've received and the blame for all you've failed to get. That means you operate by works instead of grace, no matter how many faith books you have.

Understand that you are only what you are because of God in you. Faith is simply the channel God pours into. Belief and faith are what holds the walls together until God comes. God is the Source of *all* blessings. He didn't create the force of faith to take His place. Faith is simply the power to believe in Him and the rest is up to God.

Peter then said to add virtue to your belief.

Discernment With Virtue/Inner Strength

Virtue means inner strength. We know Peter is speaking of spiritual strength, as physical strength means very little in the supernatural.

The opposite of inner strength would involve being led by your head, by weakness, crumbling under persecution, being influenced by the opinions of others, and so on. In other words, weakness leans to others for guidance.

Inner strength has learned the Word of God, the character of God, and how to hear from God. Inner strength knows how to draw from the appropriate reservoir to get the job done!

We are to add to our faith the inner strength to act upon it. But Peter doesn't stop there. He exhorts us to blend spiritual knowledge with our strength.

Discernment With Knowledge/Knowing

I love that word! When you know something, no one can take it from you. But if you're confused, you'll listen to every opinion that comes along.

To be effective, knowledge must be added to inner strength.

When we think of knowledge, we usually think of accumulating facts from books, theories, and experiences. But I want you to also consider knowledge as a spiritual know-how.

When we have inner, spiritual strength, then spiritual knowings will come strongly. With it will come the know-how and the know-when!

In Nehemiah 4:11, Nehemiah's adversaries made a plot to steal his knowing ability. If the adversaries could succeed in doing this, they could mix in among Nehemiah and the people, slay them, and cause the building of the wall to cease. This was all based on their ability to steal or darken Nehemiah's knowing ability.

But Nehemiah had great inner strength. He kept his spiritual knowing, and the people built the wall with one hand, with a sword in the other hand.

As I've stated before, keep your knowledge of the Word sharp. Then apply what you've learned to develop your spirit. That's how dullness leaves and knowings come.

Discernment With Temperance/Soul-Taming

Verse 6 of Second Peter, chapter 1, begins, **And to knowledge temperance....** Peter calls it temperance; I call it self-control or soul-taming.

When your spiritual knowing is working, your soul must be harnessed to follow it. If your emotions act one way and the direction of God is in another, you'll be an emotional weirdo.

One of the greatest exercises in developing discernment is learning to hold to what you've picked up. The soul constantly tries to confront and challenge you into not sticking with what you've discerned.

If you let go, you'll lose your know-so.

You can only overcome the soul with faith, inner strength, and knowledge. Once you've learned and developed victory over the temptation to let go, it'll become easier and easier to stick to the truth you've discerned.

When I first began in the ministry, I was scheduled to speak at a particular church. Before I went, someone called me and said, "Do you know what kind of church you're going to?"

I said, "Well, as far as I know, the church is good."

Then the person said, "But Roberts, I need to give you the scoop." They began with their list of problems they saw in the church. I thought, *Here we go again.*

When I allowed that person to deposit those negative comments, I began to feel uneasy about this church — and I hadn't even been there yet! My soul was beginning to get involved.

Immediately I went to prayer and said, "Father, I thought You told me to go. So, what is all this I've just heard?"

Instantly the Spirit of God spoke to my spirit and said, "I didn't tell you those things. I told you to go." And that was the cutting edge and deciding factor between my soul letting go and my spirit holding on.

In developing discernment by the Spirit to know a ministry, a situation, or even an individual, be careful that the words of men don't get mixed in with the Word of God. If they do become mixed, then what you've heard from the Lord or what you've sensed by the Spirit will become confused.

I knew I had to make a decision about going to that church. I reaffirmed that the Spirit of the Lord told me to go. It didn't matter what was happening in the natural or what a person said. The Spirit of God told me to go and I stuck with that.

When I got to this church and began to minister, I searched it by the Spirit. I couldn't find one thing out of order. In fact, we had a great meeting. People were saved and devils came out. It was great!

After I got home, I called this person and said, "Brother, you've either been offended by this church or you're mad, jealous, or misinformed. There's nothing wrong with this church. We had a great meeting!"

This person hasn't spoken to me since that telephone conversation. That's his problem, not mine. But it would have been my problem had I followed his words instead of holding to the word of the Lord!

The soul always wants to act independently from God, so you must develop temperance. If not, your spirit will attempt to discern a situation and your soul won't accept it. Or, your soul will attempt to push you into a wrong timing.

There have been many, many times that I've stayed with the word of the Lord despite what people have said and despite the hardship. The word of the Lord has *always* prevailed. It may have taken days, years, or just moments, but His words to me have stood the test of time.

That's what spiritual discernment is: *A fact that comes from heaven and can stand by itself without any natural support.* Don't allow your soul to throw a kink in your spiritual equipment!

Men and women don't fall because their anointings became too great or because the devil attacked them. Men and women fall because they didn't search out or hold to the word of the Lord that He spoke to them. It's against His nature to send you unprepared. Discipline your soul and go prepared in knowing and in strength.

Discernment With Patience/Timing

...and to temperance patience... (2 Peter 1:6).

I believe that patience has a lot to do with timing. We all know how the soul hates to wait. That's why Peter says to harness it with patience.

Eternity does not measure time like we do on earth. In eternity, there are no fast food restaurants, no rush hour traffic, no one-hour dry cleaning, no drive-through grocery stores, and no six o'clock news!

The spirit man operates on the timing of eternity, not upon the soul's time limit. The spirit man never reacts in haste. Your spirit wants to move with the timing of God.

But the soul wants everything done *now*. It's impatient, unkind, and constantly thinks it has to catch up with something. If you allow that thinking to master you, you'll usually miss the timing of God. And if you're successful, it was by His grace!

There are times and seasons of God. There is a certain timing for you and what you're called to do. Whether you're in business or ministry, there are still seasons and timings for each new project.

The spirit man can discern that timing and prepare for it, no matter what things look like around you. Elijah *heard* the sound of the abundance of rain before a drop ever fell (1 Kings 18:41). He heard that sound in his spirit and he knew the timing was near.

Patience is a spiritual force that can keep you from jumping out ahead of God — even when you've seen something in the Spirit. If you jump out ahead, you'll be on your own. All your own abilities and strengths will have to be used to get the job done. You'll work yourself into a burnout because you attempted a spiritual mission in the flesh. Then you get mad at God because what you saw isn't working.

It's not God, it's you. You saw it but then didn't have the spiritual maturity and patience to discern the accurate timing for it.

Spiritual equipment only operates effectively when you're in the correct timing of God. The proper equipment is for the proper timing. It's almost like the right timing oils your equipment. There's not an experience on earth greater than hitting the right timing of God! In that timing, everything works, everything comes together, and the victory is an all-time high.

God is a good steward over His timing. He is investing in your training for the appointed day. And when that day comes, your equipment can handle the task before you. So patiently wait and prepare for the accurate timing of God. It'll keep your discernment sharp. Then when the spiritual hour comes, you'll be ready to rise and meet it.

Discernment With Godliness

...and to patience godliness (2 Peter 1:6).

Godliness is not a holier-than-thou attitude. Instead, godliness is walking in the understanding of righteousness. It's operating in your godly authority and with the blood of Jesus. Godliness is walking in no less than the same ministry as Jesus did while on earth. In fact, we are to complete what He started. That means we should think like Him, act like Him, and operate like Him in the earth.

Self-righteousness produces a works-minded holiness. Ladies, God doesn't care if you wear your hair in a bun or cut it to your ears! If you're going to live that self-righteous, then don't stop at half of it — go all the way. Do like the women of Bible days and wear a veil over your face. Don't even think of showing your face in public.

Some believers are too self-righteous to have fun at church. They think the church building is holy and that it's blasphemy to eat or have church fellowship in the building.

Well, if you think like that, then don't stop there. Carry on with all the Word. In Bible days, the people couldn't even use the restroom inside the temple. They had to go out and dig a hole, take a bath, and then return to hear the sermon. If you're going to be one of those self-righteous ones, then don't use the bathroom at church. Don't be self-righteous in part; go all the way. We'll have your shovel packed and ready for you at the door!

The point I'm trying to make is this: Holiness has nothing to do with self-righteousness. If eating pork is a sin to you, then don't eat it. But don't try to push your self-convictions upon others. First Timothy 4:4,5 says we're free to eat whatever we want, as long as we pray and sanctify before we swallow! If there is no absolute mandate in the Word for your self-convictions, then keep them to yourself. Pushing them upon others makes you appear self-righteous.

I heard of a female preacher who publicly condemned any minister who watched movies or gave illustrations from movies in his or her sermons. Now this wasn't a preacher from the backwoods Pentecostal circles. She's one that's been around, but she's wrong.

This preacher said people who watched movies weren't living holy. The sad thing was the condemnation that was heaped on the thousands of people who listened to her. They were subjected to her self-righteous judgments. Maybe it's sin for her, but it's not a sin for the family of four who watch "The Sound of Music"!

I wonder what planet this preacher lives on? On planet earth, God has given us natural refreshment *and* spiritual refreshment. We have both. It's true that you have to pick and choose your entertainment; many movies are far from wholesome. It is true that you must protect the gates of your eyes and ears. Whatever enters into them will become lodged in your mind, eventually affecting your thinking and outlook. But good, wholesome entertainment is refreshing!

Everyone who knows me *knows* that my favorite show is "I Love Lucy." I think I've collected almost every episode that Lucy has made! To me, that red-headed woman is hysterical, and I receive good doses of natural refreshment from her! When my natural man is refreshed, my inner man is even sharper and clearer. If you don't allow yourself some wholesome natural refreshment, you'll become warped in your discernment and in your general outlook.

When a person is genuinely godly, it produces a spiritual awareness and discernment that is so keen, the power of it can't be described in mere words.

Why? Because godliness, or holiness, is separation unto God. It's being so in love with God that you wouldn't do anything to grieve Him. God is your best friend. Above all else, you will listen to Him and follow His Word. He'll show you how to live, and that's the main thing you're concerned with.

A person who walks in true godliness understands that revival begins personally with themselves. It doesn't matter what brother "church-politician" does, or what sister "points-her-finger" says. Godliness is a personal, intimate thing between you and God. It will lift you so high above troubles, calamities, principalities, and powers that you'll see them from miles away. Why? Because they don't dare come any closer to you! It's from that kind of godly intimacy that revolutionary power is born to change the nations.

Discernment and Brotherly Kindness/Forgiveness

And to godliness brotherly kindness... (2 Peter 1:7).

When Peter says that brotherly kindness must be added to godliness, he was going a little deeper than patting someone on the back. Peter was referring to offenses and unforgiveness.

Offenses are the number one silent killers of discernment and Spirit life.

A pastor friend of mine states that offenses are the AIDS virus of the spirit. Think about that. Offenses are very similar to AIDS. The particular offense that's slowly killing you may have come from several different encounters. It may have been harboring for several years before it will positively reveal itself. It came from an intimate experience with someone who was obviously infected himself/herself. Once it gets inside of your spiritual bloodstream, your immunities get very low.

You are now unable to fight against calamities that the disease of offense has produced. It will spread to destroy your heart, your mind, and even your respiratory system, or the very breath and witness of God through you to the earth.

It'll even make you feel sorry for others infected with the disease of offense. You'll take up a cause with them and protest against those who don't understand why you've chosen this way of life and why you dropped out of the race.

There are volumes of books written on unforgiveness. If you've been a Christian for more than a day, you've probably had the opportunity to operate in forgiveness!

The main point I want to bring up about unforgiveness is this: A person can only operate with an offense if they're still living in and thinking about the past. Unforgiveness and offenses are not a present or future thing. They are found in past events.

God doesn't operate by the past. With God, the moment is new and fresh. God wants to keep us constantly challenged in the present, always reaching for the future.

The devil has an embarrassing future waiting for him. He's powerless to do anything about it. But the devil gets power in your circumstances *today* by causing you to live in the *past*. And you can only have bitterness, strife, and unforgiveness if you're still thinking about the past.

If I'm operating in the present, I can't think about what happened an hour ago. If I'm reaching for the future, I can only *learn* from the past, not *live* in it.

If you're living in the past, then your discernment stopped there as well. Everything and everyone you view will be based on past experiences. If you know a person drowning in an offense, then you'll notice their discernment is harsh, judgmental, and many times inaccurate.

I once knew a person who was always grieved. I would ask this person, "How are you doing?"

This person would always answer, "Oh, Brother Roberts, I'm grieved, I'm grieved."

At first I thought the person was picking up another's sorrow and needed to pray it out through intercession. But after four or five times of greeting me with the same statement, I realized the problem was deeper.

So I asked the Lord about it. I soon realized this person was viewing everything from their own wounded spirit. In fact, the person was a walking, talking hurt and offense! Everything was being led by and discerned from this hurt and wound.

Did you know that even very moral people, successful at overcoming various temptations, fall with offenses? Why? Because they never learned how to cut the hurt out of their lives.

If an urgent correction is not made, a person who views everything from a wounded spirit will soon become captivated by it. That's when the devil has a party with them. He'll use them in every faultfinding scheme there is. Many churches are split apart from faultfinding people. These are the same people who have become so ravished with unforgiveness that now they've become a captive to it. They're looking out of the shattered, cracked window of their soul and emotions and calling it discernment.

In Matthew 18:7, Jesus said that offenses would come. That's not a promise we'd like to stick on our refrigerators, but at the same time it's an absolute truth as long as we're in the world.

We've all been hurt and disappointed. There was a time when I was so disappointed in a situation that my soul actually ached. But disappointments, hurts, and offenses are not the issue. Jesus said these things would come. So a sign of maturity is not how many times you've been hurt, but how fast you go through the offense and recover.

When you face disappointment, don't run from your answer. You can do that by constantly rehashing the past. Instead, run to God. Run to the good fellowship of sharp believers. Run to the power of the Word. Run to the throne of God through prayer. Lay it all before Him and leave it there for Him to handle. Run to the Holy Spirit and call on Him for truth and action as your Comforter of defense. Then get up and come through!

Many times you don't feel like forgiving at all. But in a desire to be obedient to the Word of God and receive His favor, you forgive as an act of your faith. Years ago, I heard someone say why God honors forgiveness by faith.

This person was feeling badly because they still felt like punching the person, even though they forgave by faith. Suddenly the Spirit of God spoke to their heart and told them the forgiveness was received. Then He said, "Do you know how many of My children won't forgive at all?" He went on to explain that it was such a joy to His heart for a child who *wanted* to forgive, even if they didn't feel it at the time. That's why He counted it as done and the supernatural healing began within them.

You're a silly parent if you wait for your child to *feel* like cleaning his room. We all know that day rarely comes! But when the child cleans his room, knowing that it's pleasing to you, that child will get the just reward. Afterwards, the child will be thrilled he acted on a principle instead of a feeling! The same is true with the principles of God.

If you'll develop your inner man in that fashion, then your discernment equipment will operate accurately. Don't be guilty of mismanaging your equipment by discerning out of a personal offense or problem. Don't allow the devil's schemes to warp your spiritual abilities and privileges. Learn to master offenses; then go on with your destiny.

Discernment and Charity
(Divine Love, Not Soulish "Luv")

...and to brotherly kindness charity (2 Peter 1:7).

Many Christians are out in left field when it comes to the subject of love. They think differing opinions, absolutes, no-compromise understandings, or at times kicking your tail means that love is not present. In a way they're correct. If you're standing for the laws and blessings of God and you respond in any of the above ways, soulish love was kicked out the door!

God never meant for us to have a warped definition of love. He never meant for believers to walk in the soulish abuse and misuse of it. He knew that unbelievers would walk according to their senses and lusts, but He never meant for His people to operate that way.

Do you know what charity, or agape love, is?

Let's get basic and build from that. The Bible says that God is love. (See 1 John 4:8.) That means that God, as a Being, is love. Love means God and God means love.

If the Being, character, and personality of God are love, then the definition for love can't come from your own fleshly or soulish ideas. To find out what love is, you must search the Word and see what Jesus said to a variety of people in many different situations. You must study the way He responded or reacted.

God meant for us to learn from the life of Jesus in order to know Him. He meant for us to accept the spiritual strength in agape love, then learn to operate from that point of view. Anything less than agape love is man-made, political, or sensual.

It really bothers me when people flippantly state, "God is love." Usually those are the ones who think spiritual laws are for the Old Testament. They think everything goes and whatever happens is okay with God.

Those people don't have the power to heal a headache! *It is true that the love of God is unconditional, but His blessings are not.* Unconditional love means He'll always love you, but He'll never violate His Word to give you a blessing. The choice is yours to obey.

What Is Unconditional Love?

To understand how the love of God operates, you have to know the character of God and the laws of heaven. Though His love is unconditional, it has a direct purpose. God loves enough to pull back when He's violated; to say no; to rebuke, correct, or curse a hindrance to the plan of heaven; to speak the truth in faith and hope; to bless and to give. At times God's love can seem tough because we've had such a warped and soulish understanding of what love really is. Like the prodigal son in Luke 15, if you willfully reject the ways of God, He will let you hit rock bottom — but He'll be there with a clean robe when you repent and return.

If Jesus commanded us to love, then agape love is not an emotion. As with all commands, it is a choice to obey or not to obey. You can obey God and walk in the supernatural strength and determination of love, or you can disobey and view every answer from the weak and worldly concept of love. Only agape love produces eternal, life-changing results. Soulish love only pats, or shields with a band-aid effect. We are to love out of the strength of our inner man with one goal in mind: to fulfill the purpose of God.

Love is also connected with the truth, and only truth that is known will set people free. Many believers have really hurt themselves with a weak-kneed philosophy on unity. It's all based on a soulish love they say is of God. This kind of unity takes the hot and the cold, blends it together, and produces lukewarm. And you know what God does with lukewarm things: He spews them out of His presence! (See Revelation 3:16.)

You cannot have unity if you sacrifice truth.

Spiritual Unity Can't Compromise

I didn't say you couldn't have distant acquaintances with this unity. It's good to acknowledge and respect those who know that Jesus is the only way to heaven. But if you want more of God and that's as far as they choose to go, your fellowship will end there. There is no intimate fellowship, on-going relationships or unity if you compromise a truth to have it. If you try it, you'll be setting yourself up for deception or heartache.

True spiritual unity is when common destinies bring you and another person or ministry together. You shake hands and keep on running. You never have to stop or take a side road to understand their viewpoint. You're both running on the same path, believing the same way and focused on the same goals.

Don't be deceived. You won't have the same goals if you believe differently. If you believe in praying down demonic strongholds over an area, but another thinks the answer is love through psychological counseling — you won't have spiritual unity. If you have to compromise speaking in other tongues in order to work with someone who doesn't believe tongues is for today — you are headed for disaster.

Godly love knows where the truth stands and uses it to cut through confusion. The truth of God doesn't stop at the problem; it answers with a solution.

If you operate in or compromise with any less, you're not operating in the love of God. You can try to call it that, but you're operating in soulish weakness and it will dull your discernment. You're being led by easy, nonconfrontive attitudes instead of by the strength of your spirit. If that's how you want to conduct life, then you'll constantly be putting the pieces back together, playing religious politics and walking on eggshells.

There are peacekeepers and peacemakers. Peacekeepers compromise the truth for a temporal unity. Peacemakers stand for truth and create unity. Jesus was a Peacemaker. His goal of love had direction and faithfulness. It had the ultimate purpose of bringing people into the fullness of heaven. Godly love takes your focus off of people and places it towards the goal of God. Your actions are motivated by the eternal reward, not by the temporary one.

The love of God keeps you in for the long run, not the short sprint. It is the dividing factor of the cutting edge.

The Difference Between "Being" and "Good Ideas"

Understanding these building blocks of a spiritual blueprint, Peter continues in verse 8 of Second Peter, chapter 1:

For if these things be in you, and abound, they make you that ye shall neither be barren nor unfruitful in the knowledge of our Lord Jesus Christ.

Notice that these spiritual principles must be *in* you — not around you, not just preached to you, not read by you, or thought about from time to time. They must be *inside* of your being.

When something is on the inside of you, it becomes a part of you. When these things are a part of you, they will abound, or cause your life to increase.

Notice Peter said that *they*, or these principles we've discussed, will increase you. The Word promises that you will never be without blessings, abundance, and favor. You'll never be barren or unfruitful.

A good idea will work as long as your physical, emotional, and financial energies last. But when spiritual truths are a part of your being, increase automatically happens. How? People find the answers to their problems by just being in your presence. The Bible records that many were healed when Peter's shadow passed by them. (See Acts 5:15.) People will want to hear from you and be around you, because God enriches their lives through your presence.

When truth is a part of your being, wisdom abounds. You'll easily discern between the will of God and the good ideas that constantly bombard your success.

And here's a very important point: If these principles abound in you, you'll never be spiritually blind.

Spiritual Blindness

In verse 9 of Second Peter, chapter 1, Peter warns:

But he that lacketh these things is blind, and cannot see afar off, and hath forgotten that he was purged from his old sins.

Peter nailed it in this verse: If you don't want more of God, you're backslidden! Why would a person stop at the mere knowledge that Jesus saves? If they truly realized what they were saved from, why wouldn't they want more and pursue the Spirit of God?

The only reason people don't pursue these spiritual qualities is because they've forgotten what they've been saved from. That's why people are afraid to witness and talk about Him; that's why they don't walk the walk; and that's why they won't develop themselves into spiritual increase — they've forgotten how much they need Jesus. They've grown comfortable. They like where they are and don't want to put out any effort to change. They have forgotten the condition Jesus found them in. They've forgotten how they looked before the Spirit of God cleansed them.

The Amplified Version of the same verse says:

For whoever lacks these qualities is blind, [spiritually] shortsighted, seeing only what is near to him, and has

become oblivious [to the fact] that he was cleansed from his old sins.

This version explains spiritual blindness as being short-sighted, or in other words, seeing what is obvious. In the natural, you can be declared legally blind, yet still see shapes, shadows, and colors. It's just that everything is fuzzy and objects aren't clear unless the person is right up next to them. That's what spiritually blind means in the spirit realm.

When someone is spiritually blind, they can't discern the hidden secrets, the anointings, the moves of God, and such, because they haven't developed the spiritual character to fortify their discernment. Spiritual maturity only comes by paying the price. It's not something that can be caught in a meeting. It's not handed down from past generations. It's only learned if it has been worked and applied in your life.

When a person is blind in the natural, they need help. They become dependent on other people or other things to help them get through. God gave us all five senses so that we could live a full life. When one of those senses is not working properly, there's a deficiency or a handicap.

Again, it's the same in the Spirit realm. If you can't hear God, then you're spiritually deaf or dull in hearing. When you can't discern, you're spiritually blind. That's a handicap in the Spirit.

Spiritually blind people don't have a clue what to look for, because their equipment is rusty. Even if they saw something, they wouldn't know what it was! You can't label something you haven't paid the price to experience.

We've already discussed how people misinterpret Second Corinthians 4:4. But there is another point that Scripture brings out other than identifying Satan as **the god of this world.** It also says that he blinds the minds of those who believe not, lest they should see the light of the Gospel.

Spiritual blindness keeps you from receiving the first message of Christ, then it tries to hinder the light that brings revelation and growth to your new birth.

As long as you're in this world, spiritual blindness will try to creep in on you. Satan will always be scheming to stop you in one area or get you to cease being diligent in another area. His goal is to keep you dull so you will be discouraged with God and yourself.

Open Your Eyes!

Psalm 146:8 promises us:

The Lord openeth the eyes of the blind: the Lord raiseth them that are bowed down: and the Lord loveth the righteous.

If you're not walking in patience, therefore missing the timing of God, you'll be bowed over and depressed. If you're not walking in the virtue or inner strength to apply what you believe, then you're intimidated and bowed over with inferiority. You need to be raised. If you are eaten away with unforgiveness and offenses, then you are critical and judgmental. You wouldn't know the hand of God unless He struck you. You need your spiritual eyes opened. You need to be raised as well.

If you are stopping short from faith, virtue, knowledge, temperance, patience, godliness, brotherly kindness, or love, then there's a spiritual deficiency in your life. God wants to raise you up into the high places so you can see once again.

171

Psalm 119:18 says, **Open thou mine eyes, that I may behold wondrous things out of thy law.**

The Word will continue to open your eyes and lift you into discernment. Don't ever allow the Word to become dull to you. Sometimes you can read the Bible and not get a thing out of it. You're still being faithful to read it, but it doesn't bring light and life to you.

That's spiritual blindness trying to creep in upon you. If you allow yourself to continue in that vein, you could become hardened and backslidden. David prayed that God would open his eyes, obviously his spiritual eyes, so that he could walk in knowledge and revelation.

Lift up your head, pull the life of God up and out from your spirit and hit that thing! See it and label it. Command spiritual darkness to go from you.

If you'll give yourself to the spiritual wisdom in Second Peter 1:1-9 and apply it, it will produce an unbeatable strength within you. Then no matter what comes your way, these attributes will take over in the midst of adverse situations and cause you to ride on the high places with God — every time!

testing or trying the spirits

Prove all things; hold fast that which is good.

1 Thessalonians 5:21

This chapter is not only going to be fun, but also vital and revealing. Contrary to the belief of many, proving all things is an active part of the believer's life!

I like the first three words of this verse: **Prove all things.** Notice that Paul commands *you* to prove all things and hold to that which is good. What do you do with the bad? Kick it out and don't allow it to have any influence over you!

Unfortunately, many people get a religious mentality and think if you judge, scrutinize, or critique a situation, you are of a wrong spirit.

No, *they* are being influenced by a wrong, passive spirit.

All through the Bible we are strictly commanded to judge, prove, scrutinize, and critique everything we hear or see, that we may not be deceived in these last days! We are coming into the days when, if you don't spiritually discern, you will not be able to tell the difference between the moves of God and the manifestations of the devil. You'll never be able to recognize them in the natural. They must be spiritually recognized.

It's very important to train yourself how to judge, test, or try a spirit. There's a way to do it without becoming critical, and I'm going to address that in this chapter.

Testing Is a Command, Not an Option

In some areas of the world, even in America, anyone could go into a region, say they're of God, start a work, and they'd have a following! Some are legitimate, but some are illegitimate and operate by familiar spirits. It's amazing how many people will follow the false ones.

Some people don't care if a person calls himself a prophet and rarely has any accuracy — just so their region has a prophet! That's all they care about. They're so spiritually starved or rebellious that they'll "eat" anything this person shovels out. There's a sad day coming for the people who follow false prophets. Because they didn't test or try the spirits, they'll get hurt — or awaken after a great destruction.

You need to wake up before disaster bites you!

Everyone should have the ability to test or judge what's in front of them. You should enjoy being a light among Christians and the world, but you should be able to understand whatever is before you.

First John 4:1 gives us a New Testament command,

Beloved, believe not every spirit, but try the spirits whether they are of God: because many false prophets are gone out into the world.

When John said, "Christians — don't believe every spirit," that was a command. If we are Spirit-led people, that means we are dealing with the spirit world. Everything that comes to you in a spiritual context should be tested.

Not one angel of God will ever get angry at you for testing them. You will not grieve the Spirit of God in a campmeeting, in a heavy anointing — anywhere — if you test Him. The Spirit of God and the Word of God *always* agree. So neither one of them will leave if you're testing. You're following a command!

If someone gets mad, it's a good sign something is wrong.

I've had various people come into my meetings and be taken back by what they saw. The Spirit of God would come in real strong and the prayer line might be dramatic, and some of these people weren't used to it. They might be coming from a more formal, denominational church.

I remember one couple in my prayer line. When I got to them, I could tell they were having trouble receiving. I asked, "Is there a problem?"

They replied, "We're trying to sort all this out and see what's happening."

That was great with me. I told them to keep standing there and test it against their Word level. If they wanted me to come back and pray for them, I would. If not, they could go ahead and sit down. After a few minutes, they sat down. I'm sure God honored them trying to test it all and, as a result, helped them at the spiritual level they were on.

If you're not sure about something, then go home and find it in the Word. Once you find it, go back the next night with a heart wide open to receive!

Some Christians believe everything they hear. They don't test it at all. If it has *King James* verbiage to it, they automatically think it's God. If it appears spiritual, they think it's the Holy Spirit.

I've heard them whine, "Brother Roberts, it looked anointed!" No, it just looked mystical, so you thought it was God.

The only people who believe every spirit are the ones who have never developed their own discernment.

When John said to "try" the spirits, he meant to determine the source of them. That means that all spirits are not from God, even if they say good things.

Notice John says "many" false prophets are in the world. But the word "many" does not mean "all."

Being raised in what I call full-blood Pentecostalism, I've seen a lot of things. There's an old cliché that says: You don't throw out the true because of the abuse from a few. Just because there's the counterfeit doesn't mean you should be scared of flowing with the legitimate.

Some churches or ministries will not even allow prophets or prophecy in their churches. They say they don't want the wrong thing to be turned loose. Well, as a leader you need to get in there and find out about prophets so you can know what is among you. Develop your discernment ability so you can have the knowledge of how to work with it. Shut down the wrong and work with the right. If there are false ones, then there must be real ones. Work with the real ones and receive them. Scream "no!" at the false ones and run from them.

You don't shut down the prophetic movement, certain ministries, or prophecy just because you're too lazy to develop your discernment with them.

I'm not writing this chapter for you to be paranoid and skeptical. I don't walk around afraid I'm going to be deceived or overcome by the spirit of error. I am fully equipped daily by reading the Word, my prayer life and experience with God, plus the Holy Spirit Who steps in and says, "No way!"

I'm discussing this from the viewpoint of faith and maturity. If you want to discern properly, that's how you must understand it. Don't get another paranoia. Get a godly confidence about yourself. Set out to meet whatever faces you in fulfilling your destiny!

prophecy, preaching, and spiritual guidance

Teaching on the last days, Jesus told us what would come. He said:

> Beware of false prophets, which come to you in sheep's clothing, but inwardly they are ravening wolves.
>
> Ye shall know them by their fruits....
>
> Matthew 7:15,16

Being aware of something would mean to judge it, scrutinize it, or test it. If you don't judge it, you've disobeyed the Lord.

Although we're seeing the opening of the apostolic restoration, the world has been experiencing the prophetic restoration. Alongside of it, there has also been the prophetic counterfeit. There are false prophets, but there are also legitimate callings that have crossed over into the counterfeit.

I know some people who are truly called of God, but they're not called to be prophets. They try to operate in the prophetic realm, but do so inaccurately. They operate by public demand and not by Holy Spirit unction. That is what makes their prophecies counterfeit.

As an international speaker, I've noticed that every audience has a certain expectation. Unfortunately, many times that expectation is towards the speaker and not towards God. If a speaker yields to it, he or she will go over into performing and hype.

Years ago, I used to preach at a certain church every few months. We would always have wonderful meetings at this place.

At this particular time, the Lord had given me a series to teach on for several days. They usually conducted their services with the prophetic flow, so this teaching direction from the Lord was a different flow for them.

All during that seminar, I could feel this pressure coming from the audience. It sounded like they were saying, "We want you to flow prophetically. That's what we've come for." But I knew the direction of the Lord and where the anointing would be.

Still, the pressure from those people on my soul was tremendous! They pulled on me at the book table, in the foyer, and then unified together when I stood behind the pulpit! It was like they were saying, "We're listening, but we can't wait for you to get over in the prophetic and flow that way."

Now I love operating in the prophetic in the realm of the spirit, but not at the expense of disobeying God. When I leave a meeting, I want to go back to my room knowing I have the approval of heaven. That's all that matters to me.

Finally I stopped preaching and announced, "Folks, you keep pulling on me to get over in the prophetic and flow that way, and I'm not going to do it! God didn't tell me to do it. You might as well get into the flow that God has set for you while I'm here."

Some of those people got mad, saying I was missing the Holy Spirit.

Just because you want it doesn't mean God is directing it. When I was growing up, I didn't choose to eat liver and onions either, but my mother always made me. It gave my body the nutrients, vitamins, and minerals it needed.

If you bow to the public expectation instead of to the Spirit of God, you could begin to walk with familiar spirits or produce a counterfeit manifestation. You can get things going without the unction of the Holy Spirit, but it's always counterfeit.

How People Fall to Familiar Spirits

Submitting to the power of suggestion could cause you to reach out in the spirit realm and connect to an evil, familiar spirit instead of to the gifts of the Spirit through the Holy Spirit. Those things happen all the time.

One way people become false prophets is by continual counterfeits. They step out and begin to move in things they're not directed to do or equipped to do. They love to submit and entertain the public demand, so they feed it by reaching into the spirit realm at their own will.

These are the ones who misquote the verse in First Corinthians 14:32 that says, **And the spirits of the prophets are subject to the prophets.** The ones who operate by familiar spirits or reach by their own will into the spirit realm to pull out a prophecy think their prophetic spirit is exempt from the spiritual laws of God. These counterfeit prophets actually say their gift can pull anything out at any time. Because they're prophets, they think they can give a word to you at the drop of a pin by their own self-will.

Well, so can anyone else. It's called familiar spirits.

What that verse really means is that prophets have the ability to shut their mouths! The spirit of a prophet seems overwhelming to him, but it can be controlled by him. If you've ever been around a young, immature prophet, you might really wonder if they can control it or not! But Paul is exhorting them to be mature and assuring them they can silence themselves.

God honors prophets who don't speak from public expectation or a demand of self-will. They can move the faith of the people into a spiritual expectation, and a clean, righteous prophet can move into the spirit realm to listen. But they can only move in the gifts of the Spirit as the Holy Spirit wills, not as their inner man wills.

Mark my words. I've never seen a prophet yet who reached into the spirit realm by self-will and public popularity and didn't end up tainted, counterfeited, or destroyed.

When people or an audience think they can dictate how you will move in the Spirit, you'll find they're all kin to space cadets. They're goofy and weird, and most of them don't know how to live right. They might have the prophetic flow in their services, but they don't know how to keep their lives clean by the Word. Usually they're full of sins, lust, and worldly appetites, but they like the spirit realm. That's why they pull on you and not God. They know God would clean house by Word, counsel, and judgment. If the pastor doesn't train them, that pastor will have trouble down the road.

You have to have the ability and confidence in God to override five thousand voices that say "yes" if God's one voice says "no." Then you must stand there and not worry about an offering, another invitation, or your reputation. You must obey the Spirit of the Lord. If you ever override your inward witness on anything, you will always find yourself in trouble. Sometimes it's dramatic trouble! We all can miss it, but the key is to follow the Word and the Spirit. Neither will violate or contradict the other.

God will tell you if He is pleased with how you obeyed, but people just talk or flatter you to get somewhere. God doesn't just talk; He tells you the truth.

Your Weapons

Living right is a part of your weaponry. Holiness brings strength. Second Corinthians 10:6 says when you have fulfilled your obedience, then you can revenge and stand against the disobedience of others. When you do what is right, you then have power over disobedience. If you do what is wrong, you can't correct disobedience in others.

If you're going to be a strong, discerning believer who corrects territories and confronts, you have to live right. It must be a way of life. It is your spiritual nature to live right.

Second Peter 3:17 admonishes us to beware of wicked, lawless people so that we can continue to live right:

> Ye therefore, beloved, seeing ye know these things before, beware lest ye also, being led away with the error of the wicked, fall from your own steadfastness.

Most everyone can discern an outright lie or a bad doctrine, but it's the counterfeits who get them. It's hard for people to see the doctrines that are close to the true, but off just enough to be false.

Years ago I heard a prophecy concerning false doctrines in the last days. This prophecy stated that a false doctrine would only be a millimeter off from the true one. It would be like a grain silo that is a little off its hinges. When the outpouring flood of grain comes, even though the silo is just a little off, volumes of grain will be shot from the hull but miss the target.

It's the same with a missile silo. Years ago when Iraq was trying to draw Israel into their dispute by bombing them, America tried to come to the rescue. We had target bombs called Patriots that could intercept a bomb in midair and explode it.

However, if the Patriot was just a fraction of a millimeter off the midair target, the American missile would not intercept the enemy missile. Instead, it would land hundreds of miles away from it, possibly killing innocent people.

Unfortunately, only a very small percentage successfully intercepted the Iraqi missiles. Why? The Patriots were a fraction of a millimeter off the target. Sadly, some innocent lives were lost by the miscalculation, hundreds of miles off target.

That's the way it is in the spirit. If you're undiscerning and clinging to a false belief that's just a little off the true Word, when the power and flood of the Spirit hits, your false doctrine will shoot you miles away from your divine target — and not only yourself, but possibly others will suffer as well.

You must develop a strong desire to keep your beliefs in divine order. That will keep you in the proper position to be blessed.

Not Everything That Shakes Your Nest Is From God

As I've said, many people fall into error because they don't know how to test things by the Word. They're like little baby birds who say, "Feed me, feed me." They have no idea what they ate unless it makes them feel good or kills them!

Have you ever walked up to a bird's nest and shook it? Those little baby birds think you are their mother! They'll flap their wings, raise their heads, and open their mouths. But many times the "shaker" was a human, a cat, or a snake! Not everything that shakes your nest is God!

You've got to learn that when you get hurt or disappointed, you don't run from church or from the people of God. You don't run from the things of God for fear of error or deception! You get into the Word, discern, and become more confident in things. This is how I read 1 John 4:1,2:

> "If you believe and know Christ, beloved, do not believe every spirit. But try and test and examine the spirit, whether the one that is talking to you, trying to come over you, is of God or not. Because there are many counterfeits who have gone out into the world."

Now here's the key to those two verses. **Hereby know ye the Spirit of God...** (v. 2).

It is imperative that you know the Spirit of God. The candidates for error and deception are always the people who are never satisfied unless they're in the really deep things of God, or the ones who stay with the strained baby food of the Word. Neither of those groups of people know the Spirit of God.

To one group, God's so deep that only an elite few can know Him. To the shallow, He's so conforming that they think He speaks through a psychic on the Psychic Network. A person would really have to be spiritually ignorant to watch the psychic network and think God is there.

Don't be so spiritually hungry that you'll eat anything. You have to be cautious about what you open your spirit to. If you're not strong enough to resist and leave, then those evil operations that you're sitting under will get in you!

Here's a reality check. Just because a minister's face is plastered all over Christian magazines doesn't mean the person is anointed or even that he knows God. Most magazine marketing departments don't check out your ministry. They don't trace your doctrine. They're just interested in how much of a page you want to purchase in their publication.

A Personal Experience With a Spiritual Counterfeit

Let me give you an example of a spiritual counterfeit that I personally witnessed.

A while back, I was asked by a person from another church to attend a meeting. A certain prophet was conducting a crusade in my city. I didn't know the man, but some of my friends had him in their churches. His face was all over many Christian magazines. So I went to his meeting to see for myself. When I came in, I was given a seat on the front row.

When the meeting started, it was a little different than I was used to, but I figured that different ministries operate in different ways. It's okay to be different. But if you don't have the same Spirit, you're in big trouble.

I sat through some strange things, and then offering time came. Here is where this man did the unbelievable — and here is where I checked out!

I had always heard about these people, but I had never sat in one of their meetings. This man began to offer the people several different lines to get into — a $50.00 offering line, a $100.00 offering line, a $500.00 line, and so on. According to the amount of the gift you gave, you would receive a personal prophecy from this man.

I looked around and said out loud, "Is this real? Am I in a bad dream?" By the scores, people were flooding into these lines! I was almost amused at the ignorance of it all. This prophecy-offering line was an accumulation of the things I had already tested about the meeting.

First, I knew the Bible says you aren't to charge for anything that comes from heaven. None of it. Offerings are free will, but prophecies aren't a part of the decision.

Second, there was no divine life in the atmosphere. It wasn't because of spiritual demonic resistance. It was because this man was the resistance!

Third, all of this man's prophecies were volunteered from his own spirit. There was no unction from heaven in any of them. He was operating out of an Old Testament prophetic mentality. His motivation was according to the amount of money that a person gave.

My friends, that's complete error. That's not just a little quirk here or there. That's the total thing, and the whole group was in it.

I would say that some of these people in line were people who didn't have a pastor — or a strong one who would talk to them like I am doing right now. Others were church rebels who got mad because their leadership wouldn't let them flow in strange doctrines or familiar spirits.

I looked at the person who brought me to the meeting and announced, "I'm leaving."

The person said, "Oh, uh, well — I hope I'll see you again."

I replied, "Then follow me."

187

The man that conducted this meeting now wears a robe, a huge religious hat, holds a scepter, and sits on a throne-like chair. People actually kissed the ring on his finger the day he was coronated as a bishop. I ask, "A bishop of what?"

Now this man has a 900 number people can dial to get a personal prophecy. And he continues to have large ads in leading Christian magazines.

God Doesn't Have a "900" Number!

Don't *ever* call a number to receive a personal prophecy. There are churches who actually schedule appointments in order to give out personal prophecies. Some people only go to certain churches to get a "word." My friend, that only sets you up for familiar, occultic spirits. You're not after the true Spirit of God — you're wanting a psychic reading with a Christian label attached to it.

The gifts of the Spirit flow as He wills, *not* as you will. If you want to know what God thinks, then pursue Him yourself — not some 900 number or off-the-wall "prophetic" appointment.

I'm telling you this to get you out of your marshmallow Christianity. You can't trust everything that has a dove from heaven plastered on the front. You'd better learn to use your discernment, test and try the spirits, then know what to do with it.

Some people are loyal to their own race or culture over the truths of God. That's why they become deceived. If you follow anything other than God, you are opening yourself to deception.

If my own family turned to error, I would not support them. I have a scriptural right to say no and stand on truth. That kind of spiritual law must be inside of you. It's not to be as a terror or a religious rite, but because you want to be right with God.

You cannot be loyal to anything other than the truth of God. Promotion doesn't come from the east, west, north or south. It doesn't come from color or culture. It comes from character God approves. He is the One Who promotes (Psalm 75:6,7).

If your loyalty to God remains true you'll test, try, and discern accurately. Don't try or test from an accusing or supercritical viewpoint. Have the ability to properly test, try, and scrutinize what's before you so you can live free and joyfully in God.

why do we miss it?

Remember my 2 + 2 = 4 story at the beginning of the book? It illustrates a very good reason why we can miss the Spirit of God.

Some quench the Spirit of God because they're ignorant of how He flows or they don't like the way God speaks. Sometimes people love God, but they don't want to hear everything He has to say.

Take my story of 2 + 2 = 4. To me, it's very important to have good friends and divine relationships. I like strong, godly friends with whom I can do normal activities. The Bible says there's a time for everything. I don't always want to be preaching or counseling someone while I'm eating Chinese food!

If you try to live everyday life the way you act while under the corporate anointing, you'll be goofy and weird. You'll spiritualize everything. You probably won't have any friends, because no one will want to be around you.

Being spiritual is a lifestyle, not just a prayer line. It means to love God with all your heart, have good clean fun with godly friends, and enjoy the natural beauty of the earth He gave us.

If you don't develop friendship skills, you'll be deficient in your ability to relate. Since relationships are a very vital part of life, I believe they also play a strong role in developing discernment.

Relationships are so important to me, it was hard for me to accept what God was saying to me in that math equation. We usually miss God when He asks us to do something we're not thrilled to do.

When God shows you something, you'll always miss it if it's not quite what you want to see and you add an extra point. Don't add an extra point because you like a person and want to be in their social world. Don't add an extra point because you want to date a person or do business with someone. And just because a person has been your friend for twenty-five years is no excuse to add an extra point.

Two plus two is four whether you live in Canada, China, or America; it's never five. You can never add to what God is telling you to do. You can never rearrange what God has shown you to be the facts. If you do, you'll miss Him. It's just that simple.

Maybe God has spoken to you about making adjustments in a relationship or a job. Then do it. As I've said before, if God has shown you an absolute problem and you add an extra point to cover it up, trouble will surely come. Then when you end up hurt or disappointed, thinking God has failed you and people are no good — remember where the problem came from. It came from you not wanting to change what God said to change. The problem was found in your failure to respond to your own personal discernment.

Contrary to what some people think, it's really hard to miss the Spirit of God or the will of God. If you want to miss God, you'll have to violate your conscience and desire to miss Him. People miss God by an act of their own will. A good preacher friend of mine said that to miss God, you have to go through at least fifty red lights in your spirit! You'll have more than one warning from Him before you miss it. In His mercy, God gives you many opportunities to hit the mark.

2 + 2 = 4, Not 3

For the sake of establishing a solid foundation, I want to tell the second part of that story once again. After I learned the extra point principle, I quickly learned another.

One day I heard the Lord say, *"Roberts, two plus two is four, not **three**."*

Isn't that deep?

For a period of time, that statement also went over and over in my spirit. I would be doing what I did before — driving a car, in the office, or on an airplane. Wherever I was, out of the blue I would hear, *"Two plus two is four, not **three**."*

Just as I realized that extra points could be added for what I liked, I could also take them away for what I disliked. If I discredited something or someone because they didn't match my personal preferences, then I would take a point away from them. If I didn't keep my personal preferences in line, it could cause me to miss a vital relationship.

We may not be fond of the way something is handled, but people are different. Everyone will not operate like you. Thank God the earth is full of variety! If someone operates differently from you and it doesn't violate the Word, then they operated from their preference, and that's fine.

The only time personal preference causes trouble is when we try to turn one into a spiritual law. That's one way that religious politics entered the earth. Men within religious denominations set their personal preferences over the Word of God and the Spirit of God and called it doctrine.

Second Timothy 3:5 defines religious personal preferences like this: **Having a form of godliness, but denying the power thereof.**

Personal preference is usually more from your head than your spirit. That's why it will dull or even rob you of discernment. If you place a personal preference over what God has set before you, you may miss Him.

How? You may be lacking in an area where someone else is strong. But you didn't like the way this person did something, so you cut them off. Surrounding yourself with personal favorites could cause you to miss out.

Take the ministry for example. Another ministry may operate differently than you're used to. If that ministry is fruitful and you discount them because of your personal preferences, you could miss a blessing.

We must be careful to hear the voice of the Lord. That's where we get over into discerning the different giftings, callings, and anointings within the body of Christ. That's how we learn to discern the good and flow with it.

Many times we're guilty of trying to discern according to our own flow or preference. That's where we miss out. Discern according to the Word of God and according to your spirit. If your spirit is drawing you and remains silent, then watch, participate, and enjoy!

Willful Sin

Another reason we miss it is because of willful sin and disobedience. I've just briefly touched on this point when talking about missing the will of God. Willful sin is when you violate your own conscience to be disobedient. If you live that way, you've chosen a carnal way over the life of the Spirit. Therefore, you can't properly discern.

If God told you to do a thing and you willfully disobeyed, your discernment could be warped until you repent. If you're spiritually sensitive, you'll always have that disobedience hanging over you. Get with God and get it right. When you keep yourself in the love of God, you'll want to do everything that pleases Him.

Through my years in the ministry, I've noticed there are some areas that cause people to be dull and some areas that cause us to miss God. Let's briefly discuss two more of the reasons we miss God: Fear of man and ambition.

Fear of Man

The enemy loves to torment people with the fear of man. The fear of man is exactly what it sounds like. It is fearing what man will think and do over what God will think or do.

If you care more about what people will say than what God will say, then you are a man-pleaser. That means you get your direction and approval from people instead of from God. Your life is up one minute and down the next, because the opinions of people change like the wind.

You're always trying to please someone and act a certain way, because you have to make those people like you. You get into debt trying to dress just right or look just perfect. To you, it's very important what people think.

You're always concerned with what people thought of something you said. You might have even rehearsed it over and over to make sure you sounded just right. If it has to do with your reputation, then you're more concerned with trying to fortify a person's flimsy attitude than you are with fulfilling the eternal command of God.

That's called the fear of man.

Unfortunately, those are only a few of the problems. It can go much farther than that. Religious politics are motivated by the fear of man.

Proverbs 29:25 AMP warns us:

The fear of man brings a snare, but whoever leans on, trusts in, and puts his confidence in the Lord is safe and set on high.

A *snare* is a trap that is used to catch animals. The Hebrew definition is very interesting and revealing. *Snare* in this context is the Hebrew word "moqesh," which means "a hook for the nose."[1]

The fear of man will hook you in the nose and turn your head every which way it wills. It's no wonder this deadly fear will cause you to miss the will of God.

The fear of man will cause you to isolate yourself and withdraw. It causes you to be so self-conscious that you become inhibited as a person. If you fear man, you will have a limited capacity to operate in what God called you to do.

Fear is to the power of the enemy what faith is to the power of God. If you operate in any form of fear, you are giving fuel to demonic devices.

The fear of man is so deadly, it is actually a spiritual abortion. For example, if God tells you to do one thing, but you are afraid of what people might think or what they might say, the fear of man could keep you from doing what God has told you to do.

Galatians 1:10 says:

> For do I now persuade men, or God? or do I seek to please men? for if I yet pleased men, I should not be the servant of Christ.

Those are strong words! Paul said it very plainly. If you seek to please men, then you aren't a servant of Jesus Christ. It's no wonder you would miss the will of God for your life.

Fear of Man Versus Fear of God

To get a clearer understanding of what something is, I like to go to the Word and research the opposite. For example, the fear of the Lord is the opposite of the fear of man. Let's briefly explore how deadly the fear of man can be.

Proverbs 8:13 says that the fear of the Lord hates evil and twisted speech. So the fear of man will do evil if it receives approval, and twisted speech becomes a way of life. The fear of man will always cause you to say what others want to hear.

Proverbs 10:27 says the fear of the Lord prolongs your life. The fear of man will shorten your life because you opted to miss the will of God to please men.

Proverbs 14:26 says the fear of the Lord brings strong confidence. The fear of man will leave you stripped. A person in the grip of fear will give up his family for the approval of those who can promote him.

Proverbs 15:33 states that the fear of the Lord is the instruction of wisdom. The fear of man is training for fools. There is no wisdom to be found in the fear of man. Wisdom comes from trusting God, reverencing Him, and obeying Him.

Isaiah 51:7 actually pegs the root cause of the fear of man. Listen to what the prophet said:

> Hearken unto me, ye that know righteousness, the people in whose heart is my law; fear ye not the reproach of men, neither be ye afraid of their revilings.

Righteousness is the key word. The people who know what righteousness is will be the people who have the laws of God written in their hearts. Those are the ones who will not bow to the fear of man. And those are the ones who will fulfill their purpose on the earth.

If the fear of man is tormenting you, then learn about righteousness. When you understand who you are in Jesus Christ, it won't matter what people think. All that matters is what God thinks! Let me assure you, that's the only way to live free!

Get some good books by the great men and women of God who did incredible feats for heaven. Read the historic facts of how the bubonic plague germ died in the hand of John G. Lake. Or read Aimee Semple McPherson's life story. If you want to see some heroic men and women who stood in the face of people and pointed towards heaven, then read the Bible! Read the book of Acts! These are just some of the examples of people who knew what "righteous" meant.

Don't let the temporal, fleeting fear of man rob you of eternal destiny and right standing! Take back what Jesus died to give you. You don't have to bow to man. Mankind is just like you — a created being. God is the Most High, the Creator of all things. When He tells you to do something, you won't fail. Put your confidence in Him and be counted among the righteous!

Ambition

When I speak of ambition, I am speaking of the people who want acceptance and approval at any cost. Ambition is related to the fear of man, except it won't cower to a man. Ambition will run over a man if he gets in its way. Religious politics fall under this category, and I could write a very large book on that subject! But let's briefly discuss the deadly traits of ambition.

I've known many potentially great people who phased out before the world ever knew them. Many faded away because of ambition. You can't operate in the kingdom of God by the ways of the world. Man's ladder won't reach high enough to touch the glory of God!

Ambition always tries to gain influence by whom they know and what they've done. In their conversations, they'll drop several names of famous people, hoping to impress you of their worth. They're always talking about themselves and their ministries. To them, the trinity is "me, myself, and I." Just shake your head and *run*. These are shallow, ambitious people trying to impress you of their worth.

Ambition always looks in the soulish realm. If you look rich or like you "have it all together", they'll flock to you. If they see you with someone they want to know, they'll run to be your best friend.

Understand this. God is the only connection you need. If He wants to connect you with someone, He'll do it. If you're trying to do it yourself, then you're on the ladder of ambition and you will fail.

I've known of divine relationships that were hindered for *years* because one's ambition got involved, trying to make it happen. Don't allow ambition to cause you to miss the will of God. Ambition wants everything to happen right now. It totally works in the flesh and misses every timing that's presented to it. Patience and waiting on the Lord are killers to ambition.

Ambition causes ungodly competition. It wants acceptance and approval at any cost. It causes you to cheat, to cause strife, divisions, jealousies, and hate. To an ambitious person, it doesn't matter who is anointed; it only matters who is recognized.

Ambitious people surround themselves with weak people. They want "yes" men — people who have no spiritual fortitude and are climbing the ambitious ladder themselves. You won't ever find a strong, anointed person with an ambitious one. Why? Because there's no fellowship between the two. One is operating from soulish, fleshly abilities, the other from the strength of the Spirit. The two don't mix.

Ambitious people always live another life behind closed doors. What you see is not what they are. They think you won't know it, but if your spiritual discernment is operating, they have a stench about them and you can tell it. With some of them, you don't even need much discernment. All you have to do is listen to them talk for awhile. Then you'll know what's standing in front of you.

Ambition will destroy your ability to discern. It wants to totally override God in order to gain immediate compensation. Ambition causes you to believe that *seeming* successful and "all together" in the natural is equivalent to God's approval.

The only thing God approves of is having your spirit, soul, and body so easily yielded to the Holy Spirit that you will obey at the drop of a pin. That obedience is in both speaking the truth and living the truth, whether man is pleased or not.

Because of an intense insecurity and desire to be accepted or recognized, ambition will cause a lying spirit to come upon you. Suddenly, you'll begin to lie about yourself, exaggerate what your ministry has done (or flat-out lie about it) to look good in the eyes of those you want to impress.

Let Me Speak Plainly

Do you not know that your reward comes from God and not man? You had better get your loyalties straight. Ambition causes a deceptive delusion. While you've been caught up trying to impress man, you've been making a mockery of God.

The only thing that will end ambition is total repentance and a radical change towards trusting God. Let me warn you. God is not mocked. You will reap what you've sown. And when you begin to reap what your ambition has been sowing, it won't be a pretty sight.

I've said this before, but I'm saying it again. What you compromise to gain, you will lose forever. God still owns the top of the mountain and He owns the ladder that reaches it. The only way you can get there is by living through God's school of servanthood. And upon graduation, you enter into a lifelong journey of continued obedience. It's never over until you leave the planet. There's always the challenge to obey and perform the will of God.

The only way to be free from ambition is to loose yourself from all desire to be known, respected, and popular. Ministry is not your success story. It's not your lead into the lifestyles of the rich and the famous. It's not your guarantee that our grandchildren will study about you in Church history.

Ministry is the surrender of your life's will to help the world find Jesus. It is understanding that you are nothing without God. It is a relationship that adores Him the first thing in the morning, and breathes His worship as you sleep.

Ministry is dedicated to ridding yourself of all hindrances, at all cost, so the anointing of the Most High can flood through you. Ministry gives its life to heal the sick, bind up the brokenhearted, proclaim good news to the bound, and deliver the captives. Why? Because nothing else is as important as showing Jesus Christ to the world.

Refuse to allow the fear of man or ambition to abort the plan of God for your life.

---

[1] *Strong's Exhaustive Concordance of the Bible*, #4170. (MacDonald Publishing Company, McLean, VA

how does "dullness" come?

You may not be in danger of missing the will of God, but we all have to be on guard to stay sharp and accurate in the Spirit.

Just as some addictions in the natural can cause you to drop out of life, an addiction to heaven can cause an increase of life and sharpness in the Spirit.

When drug addicts become addicted, they cannot live without that substance. The same is true of an alcoholic. They'll use everything they have to get it. They will not allow anything to stand in the way of getting their drugs or alcohol. Why? Because they're addicted!

How did that addiction begin? Whether they liked the substance or not, the addicts kept using it and putting it in themselves until they developed an acquired desire for it. Now their bodies crave the substance they're addicted to.

That's how we need to be pertaining to the things of God. We need to keep putting the Word into us and continue to place ourselves in the midst of the moves of God until we get to the point where we can't live without the moving of the Holy Spirit in our lives.

When you become that way, any little act of your flesh will be noticed by you. You'll notice you can't get by with what you used to do. If you try it, now it hinders your relationship with God. That's called growing in sharpness and discernment. It comes from an ongoing, intimate relationship with God. Continuing in this lifestyle is how you become addicted to heaven.

Some people aren't addicted to heaven at all. They like to have heaven about once a month, or when they're in trouble. The rest of the time they say, "Let me do my thing the way I want to do it." That's called dullness, my friend. Don't expect any spiritual discernment from them. They'll be coming to you when trouble comes.

The opposite of dullness in the Spirit is a sharpness or keen discernment. How do you know if you are sharp in the Spirit? Do you know what you are for and what you're against? Can you strongly stand for the right and against the wrong?

In the last days, there will be a powerful battle between the counterfeits of the devil and the truths of God. The Church must know what to be for and what to be against. Then they must stand in the strength of it. If you don't stand for and be a part of cutting-edge believers, then your discernment will grow dull. You'll be lulled and enticed by the sights, sounds, and echoes of worldly philosophies. Dullness will cause you to be easily deceived.

Sharpness in the Spirit comes from knowing and standing on what is right and against what is wrong. The Word will give you the basic facts for each element. When you know what the Word says, you'll know which side to stand on. Then when something contrary to what you know is true comes, you make your stand, for or against.

From building that basic knowledge within, you will also develop a sharp spirit. A keen spirit is built upon obedience to the knowledge of the Word. From that foundation, your spirit then develops itself to pick up or discern the motives that cause the right or the wrong.

As I've said throughout this book, mature spiritual discernment is based upon progression. One thing leads to another. One block builds upon another. And the whole foundation is built upon an intimate relationship with God.

Remember, the blessings of God are conditional. It's His love that is unconditional. To stay sharp in the Spirit, you must keep yourself under certain conditions.

The same is true for dullness of spirit. It only comes by certain conditions we put ourselves in or allow to come upon us. Dullness has no special favorites; it tries to hit everyone. It doesn't just pop out of the sky and choose to come to your house. No, there are some characteristics that we can fall into that attract spiritual dullness like a magnet. Let's look at a few of them.

Wrong Relationships

The wrong fellowship or relationship can always dull your sensitivity to God. People usually fall into wrong relationships because they get lonely. They look for whomever will take care of that lonely feeling, then they make this person the largest part of their lives. That's called carnality.

Carnality will always make a mockery of the things of the Spirit. It's true that who you associate with is who you will become like. Birds of the same feather do flock together. As my friend Rick Godwin says, you're either hanging with the eagles or with the turkeys. The ones you're the most comfortable with identify the one you are!

Eagles can see for miles, using their radar to zero in upon a target from great distances. Turkeys can only see what's in front of them.

We all know people who are carnal. Perhaps you've been friends with someone who is carnal, but now you're pressing in with God. Well, pray for your friend. If you continue your fellowship with that person, just make sure they're working on their problem and growing in the Lord. If they do not and you continue to fellowship with them, they'll try to snuff out the spark you've started with the Lord. You'll become dull in your discernment or want to compromise the decisions you make. Never violate the godly convictions in your life.

Now that doesn't mean that you can't walk in love and go the extra mile with a person *if* they've expressed a desire to change. Hold to what God has put in you until you see the fruit of change in their lives. Problems *can* be solved and corrected. People and scenarios can change. If they change for God, then support them. But if they don't, ask God to send the friends you need.

In the Psalms 119:63 David prayed:

I am a companion of all them that fear thee, and of them that keep thy precepts.

Seek relationships with people who have the same morals, the same fervency for God, and the same purpose. If you don't know any godly friends, begin to pray for them to find you. That godly fellowship will sharpen you like iron, help to keep the attack of the devil off you, and will be a source of checks and balances.

Now understand, when God brings you a friend who sharpens you like iron, they will say some things you don't like! Iron is strong, and when two strengths come together, sparks will fly! In the natural, one piece of iron will bend into shape from the heat that's applied. That's a good illustration for us.

That spark from a spiritual sharpening can destroy you because of your prideful defenses, or it can spark you into fulfilling your destiny. There are no prideful barriers with godly friends. When a friend confronts, submit, listen, and test it against your motives.

When God speaks through another person, don't fight it. If there is a change that needs to be made in your life, make it. It's a great feeling to have been sharpened like iron from a godly friend. You'll never be sharpened from weak, cotton-candy friends. So if you have a friend who sharpens like iron, you need to thank God for him or her.

Be linked with those who want to press ahead and fulfill their destinies. Surround yourself with those who know how to laugh and bring godly joy into your life. But above all, enjoy the proper social environment and keep the Lord there.

Even when you're playing golf or shopping with your friends, be with the right kind of people doing fun, natural things. If you're going on a cruise or to see Mickey Mouse, plan your vacation with people who know how to have fun and sharpen you at the same time. Don't make your vacation religious! God doesn't have scriptures against enjoying a vacation.

You need natural refreshment to keep your spirit sharp. When I'm tired, my spirit feels dull. But when I'm refreshed naturally and spiritually, my discernment is very keen.

Don't get religious in your attitudes and with your relationships. If you do, your discernment will become frustrated. If you continually ignore this frustration for wrong relationships, your equipment will become silent.

Find out what God wants for your life and go after it. He'll send you the relationships you need to keep you on the divinely appointed road. Trust Him for it.

Distractions

If you are easily distracted from the pursuit and purpose of God, it will hurt your ability to discern. You'll find that dullness is more a part of your life than sharpness and accuracy.

We all have seasons that require us to press in and focus, but if you're constantly warring and battling distractions, there's something wrong. You need to find out what it that thing is that's distracting you and get rid of it.

Webster's New World Dictionary defines *distract* as "to draw away in another direction."[1] That's exactly what the enemy has designed distractions to do. If you keep looking at all the distractions, you'll end up bewildered, confused, and dull.

In Mark 4, Jesus tells the parable of the sower. He describes several conditions in the heart of man and which will prosper and mature. In verse 19, He speaks of distractions — the cares of the world, the deceitfulness of riches, and the lust for other things — and says they will make you unfruitful.

If you can't produce fruit, then you can't properly discern.

I've known people who started strong in the ministry, but later got into distractions. Some of them ran off into sin, and some are still chasing an abnormal passion to become rich and successful. Of course, they still keep one hand in the ministry.

That's called distraction and I wouldn't ask them to discern the color of my eyes!

To find the blessings in life, you don't have to deviate from the road God's called you to. You don't have to take a side path and chase something that's distracted you. Just keep focused and keep running on the same road.

All of the blessings in my life, both private and public, have come because I stayed on the right road. If I got off and got into trouble, I just jumped back on the right road and the blessings returned. You ought to live the same way.

Distractions lure you off your path, then dull your discernment to where you can't spiritually see where you're headed. You think you're still on the same road, when suddenly you realize you're being pulled out of a ditch.

While you were roaming in your distracted dullness, the season that was ordained by God for you came and went. You were nowhere to be found and couldn't answer when your time came, because you were off on a side road, chasing distractions. Dullness robbed you of the perfect will of God. As a result, you missed His timing.

Denounce distractions that come to steal your destiny and cause you to pursue another direction! God is the redeemer of all things, including what has been stolen from you. Reaffirm your covenant and repent for any distractions. Shake the things that snare your soul and spirit, in Jesus' name!

Lethargy, Casualness, and Looseness

Lethargy, a casualness about the things of God, and a looseness with His Spirit will cause you to be dull in discernment.

Lethargy is a sluggish stupor towards spiritual things. It is the attitude of indifference and lacks emotion. If the church building is on fire, a lethargic person yawns and says, "Oh well."

Lethargic people could care less about the move of God. If there's a revival, that's fine. If not, that's okay too. You can dance in the Spirit, jump, rejoice, and cry for joy in the presence of a lethargic person — and the person will just look at you. He'll think you have the problem!

You'll rarely hear the Spirit of God if you're in a stupor. He'd have to jerk you up into thin air and shake you in order to get your attention. So you can see that a lethargic mind and attitude are exactly what the devil wants you to have.

Lethargy is the opposite attitude from those in Acts 17:6, who turned the world upside down with their faith. If you're lethargic, everything will turn you upside down!

Casualness is an attitude that acts lukewarm and is lax towards the Spirit and spiritual laws. How does casualness come in? By closely associating with people who have little knowledge of the Word. If you continually violate the spiritual laws you've set for your life, casualness will come. You'll lose revelation and insight.

What I'm about to say might be touchy to some people, so hold on. Did you know in civilized areas of America, on Sunday mornings there are some people who go to church in shorts with bare feet?

Now I understand God looks on the heart and not on what we wear, but there is an attitude that must be corrected. In America, you only go to church with bare feet if you can't afford shoes (which is extremely rare) or you have a casualness towards the things of God. Casualness doesn't understand how to hold the presence of God as precious and sacred. Casualness sees God slouched on the throne, dangling a sandal from His toe.

They may not go barefoot at your church, but I guarantee there's some casualness that needs to be corrected. God wants us to respect Him and His presence. His presence should be sacred to us, and we need to learn how to hold it and operate with it so we can walk in His fullness.

Looseness is the inability to flow with the Spirit of God. Looseness disrespects His presence, because it has no concept of spiritual things.

Looseness is the opposite of spiritual honor. To honor the presence of God, you must learn how to withhold and wait. Loose characteristics cause dullness in discernment. A person who is loose will not know how to hold the presence of God. When Jesus comes in, looseness looks around and says, "Why are you all standing so still and silent?"

Looseness will cause you to get up and walk to the bathroom when a holy hush has entered the room. It will cause you to get mad at the usher because he had to stand at the back door until God was finished moving in the room. Looseness will cause you to sit and chomp your gum while everyone else is crying, praying in tongues, and worshipping God.

Looseness will keep you from carrying the accuracy of the Spirit. God wants you to be structured so that you can hold and carry the things of the Spirit. He doesn't want you to be a bag filled with holes.

Lethargy, casualness, and looseness in a person will cause them to remain spiritually dull. You can't discern what you don't care about. If you find yourself with any of these traits, then you've lost your alertness and passion for God. It means you're backslidden.

You've allowed something precious to become familiar.

You've lost your reason for continual prayer and made it a routine.

You've forgotten what it was like to be lost without God.

You've sought to be normal like everyone around you, with no purpose beyond your present situation.

You've become totally wrapped up in what you can see and what feels good to you.

What has happened? You have lost your passion.

Martin Luther King, Jr. once said, "If you don't have anything to die for, then you don't have anything to live for." You need to be reignited and daily filled with the Holy Spirit of God. You need to set yourself on fire!

You may ask, "Brother Roberts! *I* can set myself on fire with God?"

Yes. John Wesley once said, "I just set myself on fire, and folks come to watch me burn."

Lethargy, casualness, and looseness are not a state of mind. They signal a condition of the heart.

To come out of dullness and restore your passion for God, find what you love to do and release your spiritual gifts through it. God didn't create you to be miserable at what you do. If you sell cars, love it. If you preach, love the ministry. If you're a doctor, love working at your profession. If not, find something else to do that brings the joy of God into your life!

If you need to preach but there's no place in your church, why should that stop you? Go to the rescue missions or the street corners. There's plenty of action there. Be creative to draw the lost. Your passion will be where you can use your spiritual gifts.

If you honor God with the gifts He gave you, He'll honor you. There's no such thing as a boxed-in call of God. There's an outlet for you. You must bust out of that sluggish mentality and do what you were sent here to do.

Shake that trash off of you and put action to your desires. Grab hold of friends who have a divine passion and fire. Find a church that makes you jump and get after it. Go knock on doors and ask if anyone in the house needs prayer. Feed the hungry, minister to the poor, heal the sick, and cast out devils. Come out of that dullness and into the accuracy of the Spirit.

There's plenty to do until Jesus returns. Let Him come and find you busy, highly anointed, and working!

Heaven Is Your Measuring Rod

Don't ever be satisfied with where you are in God. Be a person who has to have more and more of the Spirit of God. Be addicted to heaven and never become comfortable with what you've attained. Always press to know more of God.

Measure your spiritual maturity against the standards of heaven, not against another person or ministry.

As a young boy, I enjoyed playing with the neighborhood kids. Once I remember complaining about not getting to act like the boy down the street. I was trying to state a case to my mother and said, "Well, he doesn't have to do that."

My mother looked me in the eyes and replied, "I don't measure you against anyone else. I measure you according to the standards of heaven and the call upon your life."

Those words penetrated my thinking and became a revelation to me. Today, comparing myself to anyone else is not a temptation. Achieving the standards of heaven is my goal.

We were placed on earth in the image of God, carrying the attributes of heaven. When you compare yourself, heaven should be your only measuring rod. Let those words become a revelation to you and fashion yourself that way.

Walking and operating in the Spirit is to live like Jesus lived. Jesus did natural things, but He always remained in the high realm of the Spirit.

I believe the Holy Spirit is changing the order of many lives.

I believe there are many reading this book who have hungry hearts, but you've allowed your spirit to be damaged because of persecution. People have mocked what the Holy Spirit has shown you. You've tried to hold it strong and right, but others have mocked the purity of God in you.

Now, because of the persecution and confusion, you've come to the place where you've even drawn yourself into question. Just keep holding, my friend! God is about to break through and make all things right for you.

Then there are some who are reading this book who have lost friendships because of discernment on your part. If you were wrong, then make it right. But if you were right, then never go back on what you've rightly discerned, or it will weaken your anointing. God wants to put you back in the right order so you can be free and at peace in your mind. Without guilt and condemnation, leave those friends to the grace of God and go on with Him.

Then there are some of you who have been operating in a mystical, religious mentality. You have no pastor, because you don't think anyone is spiritual enough to lead you. You hop from church to church, looking for a spiritual refreshing.

God wants to bust that delusion off of you before we count you among those who have been led astray. The Spirit of the Lord is reaching out to you to come under godly authority and covering. Find a local church and submit to it.

When you have trouble submitting, pray or have others pray to drive that evil spirit from you. Put your feet on the ground and awaken to your true spiritual equipment. God has more for you than mysticism, psychics, horoscopes, and false prophets.

Repent of anything that stands between you and God. Then relax and become a whole person in God through Jesus Christ. When you make a place for the Holy Spirit, get ready for an awesome change!

For others who are reading this book, God wants to remove second-guessing from you. You're still learning and working with the Spirit, that's one thing. But when you know you heard right, your head continues to torment you with second-guessing. That needs to go!

Let me pray for you:

I come against all confusion, insecurity, and occultic familiar spirits, and I break their power from you, in the name of Jesus.

I believe for divine strength to come into your heart and for wisdom to come into your relationships. May the godly direction in your life be enhanced so you can see clearly. I break any false and religious attitudes off of you, in Jesus' name.

May God reveal to you the divine destiny to which He has called you, and place you on the path to the fulfillment of it, in Jesus' name.

I pray for a strong awakening, an awareness, and an exactness of spiritual discernment to come to you, and for Jesus to become alive and real to you in a way you've never experienced before. Amen.

---

[1] *Webster's New World Dictionary.* (Webster's New World Dictionaries; Cleveland, OH, 1990)